The

Silent Prophet

By
Todd Farley

Destiny Image Publishers
P.O. Box 351
Shippensburg, PA 17257

"We Publish the Prophets"

ISBN 1-56043-005-2

For Worldwide Distribution
Printed in the U.S.A.

DEDICATION

To *Mr. and Mrs. Homer Miller*
who's words of wisdom forever echo in my heart.

CONTENTS

Afterword

FOREWORD

TODD FARLEY is a Master Mime Artist. He has not only, in my opinion, surpassed his master teacher in the art — he has also extended the art form itself with his mimeography and his own interpretation in performance.

He is a dedicated and enlightened teacher and his books and tapes are now and will prove invaluable to all exponents of his art. In fact, every kind of stage performer can learn much from him and this book if they too are committed to giving total performances, uniting the body, imagination, and spirit.

So far all I have said here is to compliment Todd as an artist and as a teacher, but, far more important, he is a devoted servant of the Lord Jesus Christ and offers his service as a spiritual inspiration to all of us who work with him or watch him perform: in either case it is impossible for any of us to remain passive in the light of his God-given talent.

This book should serve as a most practical guide as well as a window into Todd's heart.

Colin Graham
Artistic Director of
The Opera Theatre of Saint Louis;
New Covenant Church, Saint Louis.

EVERYONE'S TALKING ABOUT
The Silent Prophet:

"Todd Farley is a forerunner in the exploration of physical expression which includes mime, dance and drama used as an instrument of praise and worship."

Chuck Girard
Composer/Songwriter

"The Farleys' ability to physically respond with artistic sensitivity to the thrust and shape of musical phrase is enormous. Todd's impact as an inquiring student and at the same time a master teacher in this area finds few parallels. Any serious believer with a desire to understand the celebration of victory and the art surrounding that celebration needs to add Farley to their reading list."

Dr. Sam Sasser, Pastor
President, Fountain Gate College

"Todd is a world class mentor in the ministry of mime, combining gymnastic exuberance with dynamic power and choreographed grace to communicate Christ with prophetic impact."

Barry Griffing, Chairman of
International Worship Symposium

"Todd's ministry is unique, powerful, and pure. His desire to share TRUTH is complete love with great attention to detail and attention to accuracy. We know his example is one of excellence in every area of ministry."

Ballet Magnificat
Kathy Thibodeaux

"*The Silent Prophet* eloquently proclaims the redemption of the art of mime and gesture within a comprehensive biblical format. Artists and theologians alike will find this volume an indispensable source of knowledge and reference.

The book's wealth of information, presented in a pristine, literary style, will serve well in awakening the body of Christ to its rightful role as the channel of God's voice to man through prophetic expressions of the heart."

Pastor Larry Dempsey
Composer/Songwriter

"I believe this book is part of the restoration of the prophetic ministry that God is rebirthing in the Church today."

Dr. Bill Hamon, President of
Christian International

"This concise but information packed book clearly shows that such forms of expression as dance, expressive praise, drama, mime, and even the use of the fine arts are not the invention of the modern Church, still less the unhealthy influence of 'the world, the flesh, and the devil,' rather are forms of worship and ministry authorized by the record of Scripture itself."

Rev. Dale Howard
St. David's Episcopal Church

INTRODUCTION

The lady sitting next to me on the train had just destroyed the foundations of my existence, or would have if I had believed her. She told me that drama is improper, unchurch-like and unchristian. That statement might not disturb you — but I'm a miming minister. I have become accustomed to a certain amount of misunderstanding and resistence to the ministering arts, but to say it's sin...that's too extreme. So, I gathered myself together and began a dissertation on the biblical appearances of the arts, especially the mimes done by Ezekiel. Being on my way to York, England from Paris, France, and having another four hours...I would have plenty of time to convert her to the truth. When my lecture was masterfully finished, the woman looked at me with the distant eyes of a person who has compassion on a 'crazy-man.' I guess my explanation not only didn't convince her, it totally and undeniably made matters more confused.

How many of us likewise feel confused with artistic expressions and the arts in general? It seems you have to be an artist to understand art. When you read scriptures that are more artistic, are you confused, feeling like you'll never understand — regardless of how much the preacher explains? Why in Revelation does Jesus appear with white hair, fiery eyes and the stars in His hands? Why did Ezekiel lay on his side, burn his hair, and eat cow dung? Why did Hosea marry an unfaithful wife? I guess the biggest question is why should I care about all this arts stuff? The problem is understanding these 'mysteries'. Why should I try to understand it and then how do I apply its lessons to my life? What does art have to do with me?

I wish to have a second try with that lady on the train...the housewife, farmer, blue-collar worker. This time from the start, the very start. Loving God, that is where it all begins. Using our God-given bodies to express ourselves: to each other in a hug, to God in uplifted hands and in the movements of drama. All art is but the extension of our longing to love and communicate with God... and everyone loves...

Chapter I

LOVING GOD

IN THE BEGINNING...Genesis 1-3

Adam was created as a whole being: body, soul and spirit. He was formed from the dust of the ground and then God breathed into his nostrils the breath of life and man became a living being. A being who was to walk with God and have fellowship with Him, to love God and serve Him. A being who was to become a friend with God...and a son. It was the intent of God that the whole of man's being was to serve and love God; otherwise why would God have given Adam a physical being, if not to use it.

When Adam fell, man no longer knew how to live in relationship with God. A gulf developed between man and God. Man felt a great void within himself as he died in spirit and in flesh. As a result of being without God, man came to know death. He died in spirit and in body, for the fall was so complete that the whole man fell. He lost his understanding of how to serve and love God in the spiritual, and tried throughout the centuries to recapture this relationship. The various religions of mankind are the result of man's struggles with the spiritual. As he lost his understanding of using his body to communicate his love and service to God, man tried to recapture it through science and the arts.

Many Christians today focus only on the spiritual restoration of man's being, forgetting man's body as part of that being. God wants us to love and serve Him with our whole being: body, soul and spirit.

This study will guide us in God's restoration of the body and its communication in gesture and the arts.

LOVING GOD...THE GREATEST COMMANDMENT

How does a person love God? How does a person serve an invisible God? The following scriptures shed light on these questions.

A pharisee asked Jesus:

*"Teacher, which is the **greatest** commandment in the Law?"*

*Jesus replied: "**Love** the Lord your God with all your **heart** and with all your **soul** [and with all your **strength** (Luke 10:27, author's emphasis)] and with all your **mind.**"*

This is the first and greatest commandment. And

the second is like it: "Love your neighbor as yourself."
All the Law and the Prophets hang on these two com-
mandments (Matt. 22:36-40). (Also see Deut. 6:5;
Mark 12:29-30; Luke 10:27-28.)

Jesus said: "Do this [follow these commandments]
and you shall live" (Luke 10:28).

According to Jesus, these two commandments are the
greatest in God's Word. On these commandments the
Old Testament is built; without love there would be no
Old or New Testaments, for it was because of love that
Jesus came, died, and rose again, that we might have life.

For God so loved the world that he gave his one
and only Son, that whoever believes in him shall not
perish but have eternal life (John 3:16).

Without Jesus there would be nothing (John 1:1-18).

Let us review then how to love God by first understanding what kind of love it is that we're talking about. The
word for love in the Greek (agapao) and Hebrew ('Ahab)
suggests a love which is an act of the will, one which
finds pleasure and joy in God — a love that delights in
Him and desires Him. It is an ardent and vehement act of
the mind, yet gentle and tender.

This love is expressed by man's whole being. According
to the scriptures, there are four expressions of man's love
toward God. (Definitions are according to the Greek and
Hebrew words.)

Man's heart expresses love to God when we share our innermost feelings with God and give the Lord our joy and grief — when we praise God with all of our hearts.

I will praise you, O Lord, with all my heart (Ps. 138:1).

I will praise thee, O Lord, with my whole heart; I will show forth thy marvelous works (Ps. 9:1 KJV).

Man's soul expresses love to God when we use our whole *breathing* beings to praise and serve the Lord, praising God even when we don't appear to have reason (when everything is going poorly). We praise God by causing our appetites to be after the Lord. Our wills are toward God.

Praise the Lord, O my soul; all of my inmost being, praise his holy name.
Praise the Lord, O my soul, and forget not all his benefits (Ps. 103:1-2).

Man's mind expresses love toward God when we bring our imaginations under the direction of God and allow the creativity of God to flow through us as His vessels. Our thoughts are on the Lord and our intellect is in service to Christ. Our understanding is found in God's wisdom, not man's.

*And you, my son Solomon, acknowledge the God of your father, and serve him with **wholehearted** devotion and with a willing **mind**, for the Lord searches every **heart** and understands every motive behind the **thoughts**. If you seek him, he will be found by you; but* *if you forsake him, he will reject you forever* (I Chron. 28:9-10, author's emphasis).

*We take **captive** every **thought** to make it obedient to Christ* (II Cor. 10:5b, author's emphasis).

*Then make my joy complete by being **like-minded**, having the same love, being one in spirit and purpose* (Phil. 2:2, author's emphasis).

*The **mind** of sinful man is death, but the **mind** controlled by the Spirit is life and peace* (Rom. 8:6, author's emphasis).

Man's strength or might serves God when we use it to accomplish the things of God. Might and strength speak of our abilities to achieve something: our talents, our abilities and our gifts. When these are used in service to God we express our love toward Him, and our praise.

David, wearing a linen ephod, danced before the Lord with all his might, while he and the entire house of Israel brought up the ark of the Lord with shouts and the sound of trumpets (II Sam. 6:14-15).

David and all the Israelites were celebrating with all their might before God, with songs and harps, lyres, tambourines, cymbals and trumpets (I Chron. 13:8).

Note that the expressions of might are in artistic areas: dance, music, etc.

In order for us to live complete lives, we must serve God according to Jesus' command: *"Do this* [following his commandment] *and you shall live.*" To do any less is not to live in the fullness of God. Yet today many Christians are content to try to serve God in spirit only. It is impossible to serve God in spirit only, beause the spirit expresses itself through the instrument of the body. More importantly, God commands us to serve Him with our bodies. Paul writes on this issue:

> *Therefore, I urge you, brothers, in view of God's mercy, to offer your **bodies** as living sacrifices, holy and **pleasing** to God — this is your **spiritual** act of worship* (Rom. 12:1, author's emphasis).

> *May God himself, the God of peace, sanctify you through and through. May your whole spirit, soul and body be kept blameless at the coming of our Lord Jesus Christ* (I Thess. 5:23).

> *O God, you are my God, earnestly I seek you; my soul thirsts for you; my body longs for you, in a dry and weary land where there is no water* (Ps. 63:1).

We are to serve God with our bodies, souls and spirits; to do any less is sin. Let us therefore, study to have an understanding of communicating with our bodies so we may communicate our love to God and to our neighbor, thus fulfilling His commandment.

LEVELS OF COMMUNICATION

...Love thy Neighbor...
(Communication Man to Man)

We are commanded to love one another, to serve one

another and to communicate one with one another. This is many times shown through actions of the body.

*Greet one another with a holy **kiss*** (II Cor. 13:12, author's emphasis).

But while he was still a long way off, his father saw him; he ran to his son, threw his arms around him and kissed him...the father said to his servants, "Quick! Bring the best robe and put it on him. Put a ring on his finger and sandals on his feet" (Luke 15:20b,22).

Many times we communicate mockery and negative things one to another. We say one thing with our words and another with our actions. In these cases our actions speak louder than our words.

They detest me and keep their distance; they do not hesitate to spit in my face (Job 30:10).

All who pass your way clap their hands [in contempt] *at you, they scoff and shake their heads at the daughter of Jerusalem: "Is this the city that was called the perfection of beauty, the joy of the whole earth?"* (Lam. 2:15).

In other cases we look at the gestures one man gives to another and scorn both for the expression given. This scorn turns to sin and jealousy. Jealousy is many times at the root of the begrudging. Read Luke 15:11-31, concentrating on verses 25-30; also read Genesis 37:3-4. (Read the whole chapter.) What is the result of and reason for the scorn that is sometimes the outcome of one man's gestures given to another? How do we guard ourselves from feeling this scorn or causing another to feel it?

We as Christians must learn to communicate love and unity with our actions as well as our words. To do less is to lie and sin. We must not fear the gestures of others or begrudge the gestures we give to them. These gestures of the body are to be in accordance with God's Word, and are to be pure and holy, encouraging and uplifting one another in love.

...Thou Shalt Love the Lord...
(Communication Man to God)

We express our praise, prayer and fellowship with God through our bodies. Our gestures to God can sometimes communicate louder than many words or when words are inadequate.

> *When a woman who had lived a sinful life in that town learned that Jesus was eating at the Pharisee's house, she brought an alabaster jar of perfume, and as she stood behind him at his feet weeping, she began to wet his feet with her tears. Then she wiped them with her hair, kissed them and poured perfume on them ...Then Jesus said to her, "Your sins are forgiven...Your faith has saved you; go in peace"* (Luke 7:37-38, 48,50b).

Note that the woman never spoke to Jesus, yet Jesus forgave her of her sins. Her gestures were her confession and expression of faith. We must be careful not to judge the gestures of praise, worship and prayer that another gives to God. When judging another, we may fail to see our need for similar expression or may even bring upon ourselves the judgment of God.

> *As the ark of the Lord was entering the city of David, Michal daughter of Saul watched from a window. And when she saw King David leaping and dancing before the Lord, she despised him in her heart.... and Michal daughter of Saul had no children to the day of her death* (II Sam. 6:16,23).

There are times in which our gestures express contempt toward God or are even hypocritical.

> *Again and again they struck him [Jesus] on the head with a staff and spat on him. Falling on their knees, they paid homage to him. And when they had mocked him...they led him out to crucify him* (Mark 15:19,20).

> *When you fast, do not look somber as the hypocrites do, for they disfigure their faces to show men they are fasting. I tell you the truth, they have received their reward in full. But when you fast, put oil on your head and wash your face, so that it will not be obvious to man that you are fasting, but only to your Father, who is unseen; and your Father, who sees what is done in secret, will reward you* (Matt. 6:16-18).

> *...For God so Loved...*
> *(Communication God to Man)*

God speaks to man by:

1. The Word of God
2. Revelation (visions)
3. Drama (enacted parable) (Hos. 12:10 AMP).

In Jesus, all the truths of God were told (John 15:15). Jesus communicated God to us by telling us about Him and by being Him. He taught us in stories called parables and demonstrated truths in his actions, such as teaching the disciples the principle of servanthood, one to another, by washing their feet (John 13:1-17). God showed us his love by becoming the Word made flesh (John 1:1-2,4), by dwelling among us, by dying so we might be forgiven, and by rising from the dead so we might have life (Rom. 5). God's greatest acts of love were shown and done, not just spoken of. We, likewise, must show our love to Him and to others.

> *My commandment is this: Love each other as I have loved you. Greater love has no one than this, that he lay down his life for his friends. You are my friends if you do what I command. I no longer call you servants, because a servant does not know his master's business. Instead, I have called you friends, for everything that I have learned from my Father I have made known to you...This is my command: love each other* (John 15:12-15,17).

We are called the Children of God when we receive and believe in Jesus. We become the friends of God when we love as He commands...with our whole being, communicating man to man, and man to God, as he, God to man, communicated with us. I don't want to be just a child of God; I want to be His friend.

LOVING GOD

TRUE AND FALSE

1. T F It was never the intention of God to have the body used in communicating praise and service, only the spirit.

2. T F Adam's fall took place in only a purely spiritual sense.

3. T F Man should not use his soul in praising God.

4. T F Michal was probably made barren because of her attitude as she judged David's dancing.

5. T F Our imagination and artistic talents are to be used in praising and serving God.

6. T F We are instructed to use gestures to show we care for each other.

7. T F We can communicate our love to God without the use of words.

8. T F Man is never forgiven without a spoken confession to God.

9. T F Jesus used drama.

10.   T   F   To live a full life we must love God using our whole being: body, soul, spirit.

GROUP DISCUSSION

1. How do we express our physical care for each other without offence?

2. When do "Christian gestures" become hypocritical? Read Luke 15:11-31.

3. What do we think about the use of the body, art, talents, imagination, emotions and feeling in relation to our relationship with God and His kingdom? How do they fit in?

PERSONAL ASSIGNMENT

1. For one day list all the physical gestures you do.

2. Think of a way to show a loved one (besides your spouse) you care and love without the use of words.

3. Examine your own actions in worship to God and fellowship with people; are they honest? Are you giving your whole being?

ANSWERS TO THE TRUE AND FALSE

1.F, 2.F, 3.F, 4.T, 5.T, 6.T, 7.T, 8.F, 9.T, 10.T

Chapter II

THE BODY OF GOD

In the beginning...God said, "Let us make man in our image, in our likeness,..." (Gen. 1:1a,26a).

God chooses to identify Himself with the attributes given to man. Man's physical being is but a shadowy reflection of the nature of God. God illustrates and teaches us about Himself throughout scripture by using physical metaphors and by having the natural body illustrate spiritual truths. By using natural things, we can better identify with the infinite God.

In the Book of Revelation we see Christ revealed to us in a glorious body; a revelation of Jesus is seen, full of meaning and truth, which reveals His nature.

I [John] turned around to see the voice that was speaking to me...someone "like the son of man," dressed in a robe reaching down to his feet and with a golden sash around his chest. His head and hair were white like wool, as white as snow, and his eyes were like blazing fire. His feet were like bronze glowing in a furnace, and his voice was like the sound of rushing waters. In his right hand he held seven stars, and out of his mouth came a sharp double-edged sword. His face was like the sun shining in all its brilliance (Rev. 1:12-16).

THE SON OF MAN

"Like the son of man" refers to THE 'Son of man,' Jesus Christ, in which the Word took on the form of man.

The Robe and Sash

The robe and sash speak of the authority given to Jesus. The fact that the sash is golden speaks of the divine nature and foundation of Jesus' authority as the Son of God. The robe also speaks of Jesus as High Priest, as mediator between us and God.

I will clothe him with your robe and fasten your sash around him and hand your authority over to him (Isa. 22:21).

He [Moses] *put the tunic on Aaron* [the High Priest], *tied the sash around him, clothed him with the robe...*(Lev. 8:7).

The Hair

"His head and hair were white like wool, as white as snow..." The color white is symbolic of purity. Usually

when it is used in reference to the hair it bespeaks age. In this case, it speaks of Jesus' antiquity, His patriarchal dignity, the worthy reverence due Him. The white speaks of His unblemished holiness and His identity as the Eternal One, the Ancient of Days, the Alpha and Omega, the Beginning and the End. It doesn't make reference to Him as a natural old man.

> *...The Ancient of Days took his seat. His clothing was as white as snow; the hair of his head was white like wool...*(Dan. 7:9a).

> *Though your sins are like scarlet, they shall be as white as snow; though they are red as crimson, they shall be like wool* (Isa. 1:18b).

The Eyes of Fire

"...His eyes were like blazing fire..." The eyes are naturally considered the windows of the soul. The expression of the eyes shows the true will of man. In God, it reflects His perfect Spirit and Will, the will He has for our lives. The Holy Spirit is likewise seen in the symbol of fire. We are baptized by the fire of the Holy Spirit. For the eyes to be on fire speaks of the direction God gives us by the power of the Holy Spirit. We only receive this direction when we look into His eyes. The eyes speak of the direction and the will; the fire speaks of the source of the direction and the will, the Holy Spirit. The eyes also speak of the penetrating insight of God, searching and seeing our hearts. The fire of the Holy Spirit also purifies and cleanses.

I will instruct thee and teach thee in the way which thou shalt go: I will guide thee with mine eye (Ps. 32:8 KJV).

"See, the stone I have set in front of Joshua [Jesus]*! There are seven eyes on that stone and I will engrave an inscription on it," says the LORD Almighty, "and I will remove the sin of this land in a single day..."* (Zech. 3:9).

In the scriptures, seven is the symbolic number for perfection. Thus this scripture speaks of the perfect sight and insight of Christ.

They saw what seemed to be tongues of fire that separated and came to rest on each of them. All of them were filled with the Holy Spirit and began to speak in other tongues as the Spirit enabled them (Acts 2:3-4).

By day the LORD went ahead of them in a pillar of cloud to guide them on their way and by night in a pillar of fire to give them light, so that they could travel by day or night. Neither the pillar of cloud by day nor the pillar of fire by night left its place in front of the people (Ex. 13:21-22).

John answered them all, "I baptize you with water. But one more powerful than I will come, the thongs of whose sandals I am not worthy to untie. He will baptize you with the Holy Spirit and with fire" (Luke 3:16).

The Feet and Furnace

"...His feet were like bronze glowing in a furnace..." Feet usually speak of authority or the path we take. They also speak of our foundations. Bronze speaks of judgment. The fire of the furnace is a symbol of tests, trials and tribulations. Together these symbols speak of the judgments of God which will be executed by the authority of God.

The sky over your head will be bronze, the ground beneath you iron. The LORD will turn the rain of your country into dust powder; it will come down from the skies until you are ruined (Deut. 28:23).

He treads the winepress of the fury of the wrath of God Almighty (Rev. 19:15).

His work will be shown for what it is, because the Day will bring it to light. It will be revealed with fire, and the fire will test the quality of each man's work (I Cor. 3:13).

See, I have refined you, though not as silver; I have tested you in the furnace of affliction (Isa. 48:10).

The Voice of Waters

"...His voice was like the sound of rushing waters..." Water speaks of the Holy Spirit as He gives life, cleanses, refreshes and blesses. Water, as here pictured, is like a brook or stream. When the waters referred to are rushing, many or waves, they symbolize the power, might,

authority and position of others — or in this case, of the Spirit of God. Thus, we see a picture of God's voice which can be gentle and quiet or it can be manifested in majesty and power which inspires awe. He speaks with all authority and power.

> *...And I saw the glory of the God of Israel coming from the east. His voice was like the roar of rushing waters, and the land was radiant with his glory* (Ezek. 43:2).

> *Jesus answered, "Everyone who drinks this water will be thirsty again, but whoever drinks the water I give him will never thirst. Indeed, the water I give him will become in him a spring of water welling up to eternal life"* (John 4:13-14).

> *Your wrath lies heavily upon me; you have overwhelmed me with all your waves* (Ps. 88:7).

> *Deep calls to deep in the roar of your waterfalls; all your waves and breakers have swept over me* (Ps. 42:7).

> *...He saved us through the washing of rebirth and renewal by the Holy Spirit...*(Titus 3:5b).

The Hand and Stars

"*...In His right hand he held seven stars...*" Seven is the number of completion. The right hand signifies a position of authority and responsibility (Jesus is seated at the right Hand of God). The stars are the angels of the churches. In this case they are angels in the sense that they are messengers or ministers of God, but are human. They are the leaders of the churches outlined in the early chapters of Revelation. The scripture illustrates that the leaders of all the churches (seven indicating complete or all) are given their office and power from Jesus who holds them in His right hand. Stars show light. God is that light, the glory which they are to reflect.

...The seven stars are the angels of the seven churches... (Rev. 1:20b).

...When Jesus spoke again to the people, he said, "I am the light of the world. Whoever follows me will never walk in darkness, but will have the light of life" (John 8:12).

...God is light; in Him there is no darkness at all (I John 1:5).

For this is what the Lord has commanded us: "I have made you a light for the Gentiles, that you may bring salvation to the ends of the earth" (Acts 13:47).

The Mouth and Sword

"...Out of His mouth came a sharp double-edged sword." The mouth is the channel we use to speak. The Holy Spirit is the mouth of the Lord. The Word is Jesus. Thus this scripture could read "by the Spirit came the Word of the LORD." The sword is an emblem of the Word of God. It can save or destroy. For those who follow Christ

it separates us from sin; for those who oppose Him it is judgment and death. The prophets at times are God's mouthpieces.

...the sword of the Spirit...is the word of God (Eph. 6:17b).

For the word of God is living and active. Sharper than any double-edged sword, it penetrates even to dividing soul and spirit, joints and marrow; it judges the thoughts and attitudes of the heart. Nothing in all creation is hidden from God's sight. Everything is uncovered and laid bare before the eyes of him to whom we must give account (Heb. 4:12-13).

Out of his mouth comes a sharp sword with which to strike down the nations (Rev. 19:15a).

Face Like the Sun

"...His face was like the sun shining in all its brilliance." God is the light which radiates out. Jesus holds this light. He shines with it and is revealed to us as the source of light, which will illuminate all of heaven. He is revealed to us as the Sun of Righteousness, shining forth. His glory is for all to behold and be lightened by. We are to reflect this light and glory.

But for you who revere my name, the sun of righteousness will rise with healing in its wings...(Mal. 4:2a).

There He [Jesus] *was transfigured before them. His*

face shone like the sun, and his clothes became as white as the light (Matt. 17:2).

You are the light of the world. A city on a hill cannot be hidden. Neither do people light a lamp and put it under a bowl. Instead they put it on its stand, and it gives light to everyone in the house. In the same way, let your light shine before men, that they may see your good deeds and praise your Father in heaven (Matt. 5:14-16).

The city does not need the sun or the moon to shine on it, for the glory of God gives it light, and the Lamb is its lamp (Rev. 21:23).

MORE DEFINITIONS

God's characteristics are given physical attributes in scripture. The following is a quick reference list of the symbols used, their meanings and some appearances. This list is a generalization and is not exhaustive; nor is the conclusive meaning of every appearance of each symbol given. This list is in reference to symbols as they relate to God.

THE HEAD: the leadership and authority of Christ over all things. Christ is the head of the Church (Eph. 4:15-16; I Cor. 11:3; Col. 2:9-10).

THE HEAVY HAND OF GOD: The heavy hand of God makes reference to an ancient gesture where the palm of the hand was placed on the forehead as a sign of great grief. The palm of the hand was said to represent the heavy hand of God on a person's life. The hand represented the will and purposes of God. The head represented the person's life and whole being. God's hand was considered heavy when the situation in which the person found himself was negative and was being attributed to an act of God's judgment or punishment.

THE HAND OF GOD: speaks of the will and purposes of God. It also speaks of His power and ability. Many times the hand of God expresses the aid He gives to His children (Ps. 31:5; 89:13; Ex. 6:1; 13:3).

THE ARM OF GOD: As with the hands, the arm is an emblem of God's power and might. For the Lord to stretch forth His arm expressed the thought of God's power extending out to help and deliver his people. For the arm of the Lord to be shortened is for the Lord to withdraw His help (Ps. 89:13; Isa. 59:1; Num. 11:23; Judg. 2:15).

THE OPEN HAND OF GOD: The provision of God is illustrated in the open hand of God. This is also called the giving hand (Ps. 104:28; 145:16.).

THE SHOULDERS: the place for the bearing of the burdens of the world and of His children (Deut. 33:12; Isa. 22:22; Luke 15:5).

THE BREAST: God is seen as feeding His children and caring for them, as a mother feeds her child. The breast speaks of loving care, motherly care (Gen. 49:25; I Cor. 3:2).

THE EAR: God's attention is shown when He gives ear to our prayers. The ear represents the hearing and reception of God to the needs, thoughts and desires of His people (II Kings 19:16; Ps. 40:1; 5:1; 17:1,6,;71:2).

THE CRUCIFIXION

The following is a retelling of the events and gestures which are ascribed to Christ during the Crucifixion. It is taken from Matthew 27, Mark 15, Luke 22 and John 19. Other scripture references are indicated in the text.

Then the governor's soldiers took Jesus into the Praetorium and gathered the whole company of soldiers around him. They stripped Him and put a scarlet robe on Him. Then they wove a crown of thorns and set it on His head. They put a reed for a staff in His right hand and they knelt in front of Him and mocked Him. Bowing their knees, they cried out "Hail, King of the Jews!" Then they spat on Him and took the staff and struck Him on the head again and again. They pulled out His beard from off His cheeks (Isa. 50:6). He did not hide His face as they struck and mocked Him. He offered His back as they flogged Him. After they mocked Him they took off the robe and put His own clothes on Him. Then they led Him away to crucify Him. Carrying His own cross, He went out to the Place of the Skull (Golgotha). Here they crucified Him. They nailed Him to the cross by His hands and feet. It was now about the sixth hour, and darkness came over the whole land until the

ninth hour, for the sun stopped shining and the cur-
tain of the temple was torn in two. Jesus called out
with a loud voice, "Father, into Your hands I commit
my spirit." He gave us His spirit.

A CRUCIFIXION REWRITE

The following is a retelling of the prior account of the
crucifixion of Christ. The purpose for this rewrite is to
show the significance of the gestures and their meaning
within the events of God's Word. It will illustrate the
depth that can be added to your understanding, by knowing the meaning of the symbols and gestures used in
scripture.

The Governor's Soldiers

The whole company of soldiers brought forth the
bound Jesus. His hands were tied; He was submitting
His will to that of the people and to the purposes of
God. They hated Him with no cause. They sought to
mock and destroy Him for no reason (Ps. 69:4;
109:3-5). They removed Jesus' clothes, the expression of Himself. They placed on His back the scarlet
robe of sin. He wore on His flesh the sins of man (Isa.
1:18). On His pure and holy head were the thorns of
the flesh (Cant. 5:11). A crown made by the hands of
man symbolized the sin of Adam and the will of
man. They crowned Him with sin and unwittingly
showed Him to be our leader; He paid the price for
leadership. They put in His right hand the reed of
human frailty as a staff of authority. In our weakness,

He was to become strong. Our weakness was to
become our greatest strength, for He held our weakness in His right hand [the position of power and
authority] (II Cor. 15:43, Matt. 25:32). They knelt
before him. This action usually speaks of humbleness
as a result of the diminished stature of the kneeling
person. Their kneeling was in hypocrisy, for though
in their bodies they knelt, in their hearts they stood.
They were the greatest of fools as they proclaimed
Jesus "King of the Jews," for they assumed their
words to be false, when in reality they were true.
They will come to know this when they kneel before
their Maker and proclaim Jesus Christ as Lord (Revelation); then their hearts will quake. They spat and
struck His face, hitting Him with the water of their
life and imposing their handful of will upon His face
— the expression of His being. Spitting and cuffing
the face was considered the greatest insult. They
pulled out His beard from off of His cheeks. (The
beard represented a man's manhood.) They tried to
deny Him even His manhood (Isa. 50:6). He did not
hide His face from them, as all sinful mankind had
hid from Him (Isa. 53:3; Ps. 2:2; John 5:43; Luke
17:25; 23:18). He held His head high as they struck
Him and spat on Him. He faced their attack and
accepted it. He offered His back to be flogged and
His head to be struck with the reed of our own making. Our sins and frailties marked His head. He bore
our responsibilities and on His back, the wounds of

our sickness. By His stripes we are healed (Isa. 53:6, 12; 50:6). They took off the robe they had given Him. Now that our sins were now embedded in Him, He needed no external covering to take them to the cross.

The Cross

They led him away to be crucified. He followed mankind and pursued their needs. Although they thought they were just leading Him to His death, in reality they were leading Him to the key for their own life and salvation (John 3:16). On His shoulders He bore the burdens of the world, a world full of sin. He bore the price it would take to heal the hurts and bring forgiveness; He bore the cross of death. He brought death to the place of the skull, a place reminiscent of man's emptiness — a void which needed to be filled. The skull illustrated the death of mankind and his mindless emptiness. They nailed Him to the cross through both his hands and his feet. His hands took on the marks of our sin, forever a reminder of the price He paid. They became a testimony of His will to save us, a reminder of the salvation He gave us from out of His hands. By His open palm we were given life, a palm which bares our imprinted name (Ps. 22:16; Zec. 12:10; John 20:27; John 19:37; 20:25-26; Isa. 49:16). Our sin was driven and placed under His feet — under His authority. All things were now under his authority, under his feet (Ps. 8:6). The scars were to give testimony to this. Satan pierced the foot of Jesus with sin and death. Jesus crushed Satan's head as He conquered sin and death, which had been Satan's domain (Gen. 3:15). It was now about the sixth hour and darkness came over the whole land until the ninth hour, for the sun stopped shining. The source of light was being killed (Rev. 22). The veil of the temple was torn in two. No longer was there to be a separation between man and God. Jesus was now the veil, the mediator; and Jesus was God. Then came the death of Jesus on the cross; the death of sin, the price of forgiveness was paid. The innocent blood of Jesus was that price. His blood washed away our sins. Our names are now written on His hands. Our sickness was on His back — our frailty on His head — our trials crowned Him. Our lives were under His feet. He bore all that we are and will be that day on the cross. He gathered all mankind into Himself and then gave them all into the hand of God. He said, "Father, into your hand I commit my spirit." Then He gave up His spirit, and we with it.

Now we are partakers of His life and resurrection. His power is ours. His life is our life.

THE BODY OF GOD

TRUE AND FALSE

1.   T   F   God identifies His characteristics in sym-
             bolism which is illustrated by body parts.

2. T F The white hair of Christ primarily denotes age.

3. T F The Holy Spirit is spoken of as having a voice like the sound of rushing water.

4. T F Seven is the number of completion.

5. T F God is light.

6. T F The heavy hand of God refers to the great sorrow of Christ at the crucifixion.

7. T F The open hand of God speaks of His provision for us.

8. T F The act of kneeling is a gesture of humility.

9. T F Spitting and cuffing is considered a mild insult.

10. T F The palm of Jesus is imprinted with our names.

GROUP DISCUSSION

1. What are some of the other ways God reveals Himself in nature?

2. Why does God choose to reveal Himself in symbols of the physical being? How does this help us to understand Him?

3. Why was Christ's appearance different in the Book of Revelation than in the Gospels? What are the differences?

PERSONAL ASSIGNMENT

1. Rewrite the events leading up to the crucifixion from the time in the garden. Use a commentary and a concordance for help. Replace the gestures found in your account by their meanings. Use the retelling of the crucifixion found in this chapter as a model.

2. How is God revealed in His creation as seen in Job 38-39?

3. Do a word study on the Hand of God.

ANSWERS TO THE TRUE AND FALSE

1. T, 2. F, 3. T, 4. T, 5. T, 6. T, 7. T, 8. T, 9. F, 10. T

Chapter III

THE BODY OF MAN

Man's body was created for communication and fellowship with God. Each part communicates a concise thought. Each movement and rhythm shows an idea or emotion. Although man was so created, the fall of man corrupted our understanding of this. Now is the day of restoration. Christ died for the whole man. Shouldn't we give to Him our whole being? Shouldn't He reign in our whole being? Let us bring our bodies under the Lordship of Jesus Christ.

THE COMMUNICATION OF THE BODY

The Madman

David was running from King Saul, who had just tried to kill David by hurling a spear at him (that's one gesture it didn't take a book to interpret). David ran to the kingdom of Gath under the rule of King Achish; however, his fame went before him. The people of Gath had heard about David's killing tens of thousands (a poetical number used to indicate a vast amount). David realized he was in a dangerous position; and his reputation wasn't helping him. He needed to take action.

David took these words to heart and was very much afraid of Achish king of Gath. So he feigned insanity in their presence; and while he was in their hands he acted like a madman, making marks on the doors of the gate and letting saliva run down his beard (I Sam. 21:12).

The king and the people thought he was indeed mad. The beard was the symbol of manhood. What man in his right mind would drool on his own beard and mock his own manhood? Generally the beard was carefully groomed and a man would rather die than to be shamed by having his beard shaved. Since David could not explain with words the problems he was having, he escaped the wrath and suspicion of the people of Gath by acting mad (drawing on the doors and gates as if to bless or curse, and then denying his manhood in a way, that if he were sane, he would rather die than do). The result of his acting was that he left Gath in one piece, alive. He escaped out of the hands (power) of the people of Gath who could have harmed him.

The Betrayal

Joab wanted to get rid of Amasa, but had to catch him unaware. *"Joab said to Amasa, 'How are you my brother?'*

Then Joab took Amasa by the beard with his right hand to kiss him. Amasa was not on his guard against the dagger in Joab's hand, and Joab plunged it into his belly and...Amasa died" (II Sam. 20:9). Only the closest friend or brother would touch the beard, or the manhood, of another. The kiss was a sign of servanthood and brotherly affection. It was no wonder Amasa was taken off guard. He must have thought Joab was paying him homage — some homage.

Misunderstood

When Queen Esther revealed the plot of Haman to destroy her people, Haman fell onto her couch in a gesture of begging. Right then the King came in and saw Haman falling onto the Queen, and thought Haman was trying to molest her. With all of Haman's other crimes against Esther, this was too much. *"The King exclaimed, 'Will he even molest the queen while she is with me in the house?' As soon as the word left the king's mouth, they* [the servants] *covered Haman's face...and took him to the gallows where he was hung"* (Esther 7). Haman's face was covered as a sign that he wasn't worthy to look upon another or to be looked at.

A Shoe for Your Wife

When the widow Ruth offered herself to Boaz, Boaz wanted to marry her —but there was a problem. According to the law of Moses, the closest of kin has the first right of marriage (Deut. 25:7-10). Since Boaz wasn't the closest-of-kin, he had to get the other man to release his right to marry Ruth. He did this by going before the elders and asking the closest-of-kin if he wished to marry Ruth and redeem her. The kinsman had no desire to marry Ruth, for he felt it might endanger his own estate. So he gave Boaz the right to marry Ruth and thereby redeem her. The kinsman did this by taking off his own sandal and giving it to Boaz before the elders. This was to say in gesture "I give up my right to marry (redeem) Ruth to Boaz" (Ruth 4). The shoe was a symbol of the right to ownership and possession.

GOD'S ARMOR FOR THE BELIEVER (EPH. 6:10-24)

...put on the full armor of God, so that when the day of evil comes, you may be able to stand your ground, and after you have done everything, to stand. Stand firm then, with the belt of truth buckled around your waist, with the breastplate of righteousness in place, and with your feet fitted with the readiness that comes from the gospel of peace. In addition to all this, take up the shield of faith, with which you can extinguish all the flaming arrows of the evil one. Take the helmet of salvation and the sword of the Spirit, which is the word of God. And pray in the Spirit on all occasions with all kinds of prayers and requests. With this in mind, be alert and always keep on praying for all the saints. Pray also for me, that whenever I open my mouth, my words may be given me so that I will fear-lessly make known the mystery of the gospel, for which I am an ambassador in chains. Pray that I may declare it fearlessly, as I should (Eph. 6:13-20).

Herein we see that the life of the Christian is at times the life of a warrior, dressed in the armor of God, with Jesus as our Captain. Our foe is the devil and his schemes, and evil wherever it is found.

Finally, be strong in the Lord and in his mighty power. Put on the full armor of God so that you can take your stand against the devil's schemes. For our struggle is not against flesh and blood, but against the rulers, against the authorities, against the powers of this dark world and against the spiritual forces of evil in the heavenly realms (Eph. 6:10-12).

I [Paul] *have fought a good fight...*(II Tim. 4:7).

Endure hardship with us like a good soldier of Christ Jesus (II Tim. 2:3).

For it became him, for whom are all things, and by whom are all things, in bringing many sons unto glory, to make the captain of their salvation [Jesus] *perfect through sufferings* (Heb. 2:10 KJV).

Put on the Whole Armor and Stand

"*...Put on the whole armor of God, that ye may stand...*" The first step in preparing for the good fight of faith is putting on the armor of God; we will see that this is taking on the person of the Lord Jesus Christ, since each piece of armor can only be obtained through Jesus. The act of standing represents that the whole person is fully present — standing ready for the examination and administrations of the Lord. We stand before Him who is Judge and King. We stand offering ourselves completely to Him and accepting Him completely into our lives. Standing is also a posture of prayer. In this case it can communicate the thought of standing one's ground, prepared for battle.

Rather clothe yourselves with the Lord Jesus Christ... (Rom. 13:14).

...he who stands firm to the end will be saved (Matt. 24:13).

When these things begin to take place, stand up and lift up your heads, because your redemption is drawing near (Luke 21:28).

For we will all stand before God's judgment seat (Rom. 14:10b).

...it is by faith you stand firm (II Cor. 1:24b).

The Belt of Truth

The King James Version reads *"having your loins girt about with truth"* rather than *"with the belt of truth buckled around the waist."* The Greek text suggests this area as symbolic of the reproduction and procreation of man. In this way the symbol would suggest that our productivity in the Kingdom of God is proliferated in truth. Our work and activities reveal the truth of God to others — the truth that brings and gives life is Jesus. The waist is a symbol of life and appetite, or soul. The loins are used as a symbol of strength, power, vigor and maturity, which is to be controlled by the Spirit of God, by His Truth.

Jesus answered, "I am the way and the truth and the life. No one comes to the Father except through me" (John 14:6).

Wherefore gird up the loins of your mind, be sober, and hope to the end for the grace that is to be brought unto you at the revelation of Jesus Christ (I Pet. 1:13 KJV).

Righteousness will be his belt and faithfulness the sash around his waist (Isa. 11:5).

Let your loins be girded about and your lights burning; and ye yourselves like unto men that wait for their lord, when he will return from the wedding; that when he cometh and knocketh, they may open unto him immediately (Luke 12:35-36 KJV).

We as Christians are to have our abilities, power and maturity based in Jesus. We are to dress ourselves in Him, to give ourselves over to His ways and work, and to wait on Him as mature Christians.

The Breastplate of Righteousness

"...with the breastplate of righteousness in place..." refers to the righteousness of the believer which is given to us by the empowerment of the Holy Spirit, which is the gift of Jesus. It cannot be earned, only received from Jesus. This righteousness is given only when we repent of our sin and receive Christ as Saviour by faith. The breast is the symbol of tenderness, life and closeness to the heart (emotions). This shows that the feelings of the Christian

are protected by God's love and grace. The breastplate is a symbol for righteous living, a life in which we fear no wrong. Our lives, feelings and emotions are given to God and covered by Him so that we are protected by Him. All we have to do is accept His grace and rest in Him during times of emotional stress and difficulty.

He put on righteousness as his breastplate...(Isa. 59:17).

It is because of him that you are in Christ Jesus, who has become for us wisdom from God — that is, our righteousness, holiness and redemption (I Cor. 1:30).

...let us be self-controlled, putting on faith and love as a breastplate...(I Thess. 5:8).

For if, by the trespass of the one man, death reigned through that one man, how much more will those who receive God's abundant provision of grace and of the gift of righteousness reign in life through the one man, Jesus Christ (Rom. 5:17).

The Feet and the Gospel of Peace

"...with your feet fitted with the readiness that comes from the gospel of peace..." This tells us to have our foundation (represented by the feet) firmly rooted in the peace of Jesus and the Gospel that He preached. Jesus is the Gospel of Peace. Our Christian walk through life will be peaceful if we build it on the foundation of the Gospel and the teachings of Jesus. The fact that our feet are

"fitted with readiness" shows us that it is a state of being that we must give ourselves over to. By an act of my will, I accept the peace of Jesus (His gospel), letting it guide my life and paths (represented by the feet). The feet also stand for our paths in life as we spread the Good News of the Gospel of Jesus. We are to evangelize and be His heralds of peace.

For he himself is our peace...He came and preached peace to you who were far away and peace to those who were near (Eph. 2).

...his name means "king of righteousness"; then also, "king of Salem" means "king of peace" (Heb. 7:2b).

He has preserved our lives and kept our feet from slipping (Ps. 66:9).

Look, there on the mountains, the feet of one who brings good news, who proclaims peace (Nah. 1:15).

The Shield of Faith

"...take up the shield of faith, with which you can extinguish all the flaming arrows of the evil one..." When we believe and have confidence in the divine truths of God (the Gospel), we can not be led astray. Our assurance in Christ is a shield against the lies (flaming darts) of the evil one.

In ancient warfare there was an arrow made of a hollow reed which could be filled with combustible material.

The arrow was then set on fire and shot from "slack bows." Whatever was struck burst into flames. Water could not quench it, and only made it worse. The fire could only be put out by covering it with earth. A shield, which was large enough to protect the whole person, was used as a defense against these fiery darts.

God is our shield when we have total faith in Him. Our faith is to be extended into every area of our lives, just as the shield protects every expression of our bodies — from our head (thoughts, leadership, etc.) down to our feet (foundation, etc.). Faith will protect us from the lies that would consume us, lies thrown at us by others and by the enemy. Fire, when used by the evil one, is a symbol of destruction and temptation. We cannot win over these attacks by natural means; we cannot just throw water on the fire. When we are shielded by faith in God, the fire is quenched in the earth or dust, which is the place of humiliation. Lies will either humiliate or consume us if we take them in. Only by faith in God and the Gospel of Jesus can we unswervingly follow the ways of truth, refusing to allow the falsehood, which would destroy us, to lead us from the paths of God.

> *Do not be afraid, Abram. I am your shield, your very great reward* (Gen. 15:1b).

> *...how much more those who live in houses of clay, whose foundations are in the dust, who are crushed more readily than a moth* [expressing worthlessness and weakness]! (Job 4:19).

He will cover you with his feathers, and under his wings you will find refuge; his faithfulness will be your shield and rampart (Ps. 91:4).

O house of Israel, trust in the Lord — He is their help and shield (Ps. 115:9).

Beloved, think it not strange concerning the fiery trial which is to try you, as though some strange thing happened unto you (I Pet. 4:12 KJV).

The Helmet of Salvation

"Take the helmet of salvation..." Our helmet is the hope of salvation given to us in Jesus by the grace of God. The helmet protects our thinking, as the breastplate protects our feelings. Our covering is Jesus and what He gives. He is our leadership and our head (the expressions of leadership, thought and control).

He put on righteousness as his breastplate, and the helmet of salvation on his head (Isa. 59:17a).

But since we belong to the day, let us be self-controlled, putting on faith and love as a breastplate, and the hope of salvation as a helmet (I Thess. 5:8).

For my eyes have seen your salvation [Jesus]... (Luke 2:30).

The salvation of the righteous comes from the Lord; he is their stronghold in the time of trouble (Ps. 37:39).

...he crowns the humble with salvation (Ps. 149:4b).

The Sword of the Spirit

"...The sword of the Spirit, which is the word of God..."
The sword is the Word which comes from the mouth of
our Lord Jesus Christ. *"The word of God is living and
active. Sharper than any double-edged sword, it penetrates
even to dividing soul and spirit* [emotions from character],
joints and marrow [that which binds and feeds], *it judges
the thoughts and attitudes of the heart....Everything is uncovered and laid bare before the eyes* [which penetrate and
see all], *of him to whom we must give account"* (Heb.
4:12-13). The words which we pronounce can be words
of life or death. They are a double-edged sword, cutting
both ways. When we proclaim the Word of the Lord, it
brings life or the judgments of God. When we proclaim
evil, we bring injury and harm (as a sword might sever
and hurt). In our power (our hand), we can hold God's
sword — or sin's.

*Out of his mouth comes a sharp sword with which
to strike down the nations* (Rev. 19:15a).

He made my mouth like a sharpened sword...(Isa.
49:2).

For the lips of an adulteress drip honey [sweet to
taste], *and her speech is smoother than oil* [easy to
accept, deceptive], *but in the end she is bitter as gall,
sharp as a double-edged sword. Her feet* [foundations
and dominion] *go down to death; her steps* [path she
leads us on] *lead straight to the grave. She gives no
thought to the way of life* [she has not the helmet of

salvation]; *her paths are crooked* [in contrast to God's straight paths], *but she knows it not* [she is deceived and those who follow her are deceived by her] (Prov. 5:3-6).

May the praise of God be in their mouths and a double-edged sword [God's Word] *in their hands* [power and purpose], *to inflict vengeance on the nations and punishment on the peoples, to bind* [to restrict and control] *their kings with fetters, their nobles with shackles of iron, to carry out the sentence written against them. This is the glory of all his saints. Praise the Lord* (Ps. 149:6-9).

Please note that we do not fight against flesh and blood, but against the evil in this world and in the heavens. We, as believers, all fight in the spiritual when we praise God and glorify his Name. By praise and the proclamation of God's Word we DO bind the enemy and restrict the works of the evil one. This is the work of all of us; praise God. The power is in our hands to proclaim God's truth in our situations and see God's victory become ours.

THE ACTIONS OF THE WARRIOR

Outside of the actions which are inherent with each piece of armor, we are instructed to pray with much supplication, to watch, and to reveal. We are commanded to pray in the Spirit, making supplication and seeking the benefits of God. We are to watch with perseverance and care for the full spiritual growth of the saints. Speaking and teaching the truths of the Gospel, we must become ambassadors in bonds, being pressed by those around us and yet bold in the proclamation of Jesus Christ, who is our liberty.

THE BODY OF MAN

TRUE AND FALSE

1. T F Each part of the body is functional only and does not communicate thought.

2. T F The beard of a man is a symbol of his manhood.

3. T F For a man to kiss another man was a gesture of brotherly affection.

4. T F The shoe is a symbol for right to ownership or possession.

5. T F Standing is a posture of prayer.

6. T F The feet are to be founded in our own good works.

7. T F Water cannot quench the darts thrown at the shield of faith.

8. T F The breastplate protects our thoughts.

9. T F Our words can be as a double-edged sword.

10. T F The breastplate of righteousness is also called the breastplate of faith and love.

GROUP DISCUSSION

1. What gestures are used in the church service during praise and worship as well in the general ministry?

2. How do we look to the outward appearances of a person in judging who that person is and what he is like? Why do we do this? How does God instruct us to be clothed?

PERSONAL ASSIGNMENT

1. Read Job 40-41. How is man pictured in comparison to God? Write a list of the symbols used with the aid of a commentary and a concordance.

2. Define the symbolism of the following parts: the head, the hand, the feet, the chest, the heart, the arm, the hair, etc. Use a concordance to aid you and make your list as exhaustive as possible, then use it in future readings.

ANSWERS TO THE TRUE AND FALSE

1. F, 2. T, 3. T, 4. T, 5. T, 6. F, 7. T, 8. F, 9. T, 10. T

Chapter IV

MAN TO GOD

When man communicates with God, it can have a profound effect on the body. Man's being was created to have fellowship with God and to be a vehicle through which God can show forth His power. What happens to the physical being when it is submitted to God? Is there a visible effect which we can see today or a spiritual one that profoundly changes us?

FACES OF LIGHT

The face is the most communicative part of the body, readily showing emotion and thought. It is the house of the senses, and shows sense-related responses. It is the first place we look to see beauty. At times we have referred to someone as being dark or light. We speak of a person's face as 'shining' or 'glowing' with excitement or love. In death the light of the face is extinguished. How can this be?

Moses Shining Face

When Moses went up to speak to the Lord he looked like all of us; his face was as dull as the rest. When he came down from being with the Lord and talking with Him, Moses' face was bright and radiant. The people were frightened so badly Moses had to cover his face with a veil (Ex. 34:30,33,35). Why did his face glow? God is the source of light. God is light. The presence of light in a person's face speaks of life, health and joy. The absence speaks of death, sickness and sorrow. Moses had been in the very presence of God, the very presence of life and light.

As the sun will tan the flesh, so the light of God marked Moses' face with light. Moses was full of the Lord and His ways. I want the Lord's face to shine on me so that I might know His favor, pleasure, love and joy, that I might reflect His light on my face and in my eyes. Our faces literally shine when we worship God and meet with Him. In our daily life we can have bright faces by walking on the path in which God leads us, and by bearing the fruits of His Spirit.

When I smiled at them, they scarcely believed it; the light of my face was precious to them (Job 29:24).

You are the light of the world. A city on a hill cannot be hidden. Neither do people light a lamp and put it under a bowl. Instead they put it on its stand, and it gives light to everyone in the house. In the same way, let your light shine before men, that they may see

your good deeds and praise your Father in heaven
(Matt. 5:14-16).

We can literally and spiritually shine for God. As we
share God with others by our words and actions, and
show them His life by our faces, we reflect God's light.

Having His light in our hearts, we are to shine with the
glory of God so that people might see Jesus. We are the
sons and daughters of light; we are called to shine His
light in a world filled with darkness. We can shine His life
and joy.

*You are all sons of the light and sons of the day. We
do not belong to the night or to the darkness* (I Thess.
5:5).

*For God, who said, "Let light shine out of dark-
ness," made his light shine in our hearts to give us the
light of the knowledge of the glory of God in the face
of Christ* (II Cor. 4:6).

For the face to become pale, losing light, is the result
of the draining of the life force. The face is pale in death,
sickness, fear and sin.

His [King Balshazzar's] *face turned pale and he
was so frightened that his knees knocked together and
his legs gave way...*[He] *became even more terrified
and his face grew more pale* (Dan. 5:6,9).

*At the sight of them, nations are in anguish; every
face turns pale* (Joel 2:6).

In the light of God's face there is life, joy and victory.

Restore us, O God; make your face shine upon us, that we may be saved (Ps. 80:3).

Let your face shine on your servant; save me in your unfailing love (Ps. 31:16).

Many are asking, "Who can show us any good?" Let the light of your face shine upon us, O Lord. You have filled my heart with greater joy than when their grain and new wine abound. I will lie down and sleep in peace, for you alone, O Lord, make me to dwell in safety (Ps. 4:6-8).

There will come a time when we shall see God as Moses did. Then our faces will shine like Moses'. We shall know Him fully. He shall shine on us, being the source of light and life illuminating our entire being.

They will see his face, and his name will be on their foreheads. There will be no more night. They will not need the light of a lamp or the light of the sun, for the Lord God will give them light. And they will reign forever and ever (Rev. 22:4-5).

Now we see but a poor reflection [as in a mirror]; *then we shall see face to face. Now I know in part; then I shall know fully, even as I am fully known* (I Cor. 13:12).

The Eyes and Light

The eyes reflect the life and emotion of mankind and thereby have become the window to the soul. The eyes both send and receive information. It is in the eyes that the young romantic finds the expressions of love and caring. Hate and anger are seen in the eyes of those who feud. The eyes can shine with the light of God, with health and life. We say that someone's eyes sparkle.

The eye is the lamp of the body. If your eyes are good, your whole body will be full of light. But if your eyes are bad, your whole body will be full of darkness. If then the light within you is darkness, how great is that darkness (Matt. 6:22-23).

I am sending you to them to open their eyes and turn them from darkness to light, and from the power of Satan to God, so that they may receive forgiveness of sins and a place among those who are sanctified by faith in me (Acts 26:17-18).

Look on me and answer, O Lord my God. Give light to my eyes, or I will sleep in death;...(Ps. 13:3).

The Arms of Moses

The Amalekites were attacking the Israelites; it was the Israelites first real battle since their escape from Egypt. Moses had instructed Joshua to choose some fighters and go fight against the the Amalekites. While Joshua prepared for war, Moses climbed a hill with Aaron and Hur. Moses lifted his arms with the staff of God in his hands and the battle below began. *"As long as Moses held up his hands, the Israelites were winning, but whenever he lowered his hands, the*

Amalekites were winning" (Ex. 17:11; 17:8-11, paraphrased).

God was showing forth his delivering power through
the gestures of Moses. The uplifted hands with staff was a
gesture that had been used before when Moses pronounced the plagues and opened the waters of the sea so
the Israelites could cross. This gesture was known as a
gesture of power used by the ancients; now it became a
symbol of the power of God. In the power (hand) of
Moses, was the Power (seen in the rod) of God. When it
was uplifted, when God's will and purposes were glorified,
there was victory. When we glorify God and, by our wills,
lift His will and purposes for our lives above our own
thoughts (head), He brings victory.

Now Moses had been holding up his hands for
quite some time when he began running out of
strength. His arms started to drop and the Amalekites
began to win the battle. So Aaron and Hur found a
rock for him to sit on and, with one of them on either
side, they lifted his arms and held them for him. His
hands were thus upheld until sunset. *"So Joshua over-
came the Amalekite army with the sword"* (Ex. 17:13;
17:13-15, paraphrased).

At times we grow tired of the fight or the effort re-
quired to be strong. For this reason God gives us help to
meet the battles of life. On one side we have our Pastor or
ministers (Aaron), and on the other our church family
(Hur). If we will but submit to their help and gentle

administrations, we too, with the help of God, can be as Joshua...overcomers.

God didn't want Moses, Joshua or anyone else to forget what He had done, so He told Moses to write it down and build an altar. The altar was to be called 'Jehovah-nissi,' the Lord is my Banner. Throughout scripture, the arm represents power and might. For it to be made bare was a gesture which symbolized preparation for war. God used Moses' hands and arms as a banner which could be seen by all looking at Moses on that hill; the uplifted rod in the hands of Moses showed the power of God. We, likewise, must not forget the work of the Lord as He overcomes the problems of our lives. We should write down what He has done so that we might remember it. We should lift our hands in praise and look toward the Lord who is our banner.

The literal translation of the Hebrew in Exodus 17:16 is *"...for hands were lifted up to the throne of the Lord..."* It means that an oath was sworn by Moses and was as such, an admonition to the people of Israel to pledge themselves to fulfill God's purposes and will. The hands were lifted as a symbol of an oath. This is a symbol used throughout scripture. Since the hands represent man's power, purposes and goals, it is understandable that they would be used in a gesture for pledging oneself. When we lift our hands in praise, may we touch the throne of God with our pledged love and obedience.

The Lord will lay bare his holy arm in the sight of all the nations, and all the ends of the earth will see the salvation of our God (Isa. 52:10).

Who has believed our message and to whom has the arm of the Lord been revealed? (Isa. 53:1).

Turn your face toward the siege of Jerusalem and with bared arm prophesy against her (Ezek. 4:7).

But Abram said to the king of Sodom, "I have raised my hand to the Lord, God Most High, Creator of heaven and earth, and have taken an oath..." (Gen. 14:22).

STRENGTH IN THE HOPE OF THE LORD

He gives strength to the weary and increases the power of the weak. Even youths grow tired and weary, and young men stumble and fall; but those who hope in the Lord will renew their strength. They will soar on wings like eagles; they will run and not grow weary, they will walk and not be faint (Isa. 40:29-31).

For those who trust in God, there is a supply of physical and spiritual strength that has no end. In times past, God has provided for his people, or chosen instruments, extra physical endurance and strength to accomplish the task set before them. This being true, we can expect God to give us the needed energy and fortitude to accomplish the tasks He has given us, be they physical or spiritual. All that we must do is trust in God. In our weakness He will make us strong. In the passage from Isaiah 40, we see youth as an example of the maximum expression of human strength and endurance. However, even when we are at our best we get tired. Youth is used as an example to show us that God can meet the needs of the strong and the weak; all need His strength and renewal. To *"soar on wings like eagles"* is to be free, as Christians, to rise joyfully out of our circumstances and surroundings, looking to the Lord. We can possess our land with might and ease.

He satisfies my desires with good things, so that my youth is renewed like the eagle's (Ps. 103:5).

When we run the race of life and ministry (I Cor. 9:24-27), we *"will run and not grow weary."* As we follow the path God has set for our lives, we *"will walk and not faint."* For as we trust the Lord, looking to Him for strength and guidance, we can walk in victory, conquering and possessing the land for Jesus. We will not become weak in doing good or in following after the Lord because God Himself will be our strength (Gen. 24:40; I Kings 6:12; Gal. 5:16; Eph. 5:2,8).

Those To Whom God Gave Strength!

Samson (Judg. 13-16)

During the time that Israel was ruled by 'the judges' (leaders chosen by God), one rose up that was truly unique. He was a miracle child, born of a sterile mother by the power of God. Samson was his name. His parents were commanded not to give him wine or unclean meat (according to the law of Moses). His hair was never to be cut as a symbol of his dedication as a Nazarite and his separation unto God. When he grew to adulthood, God planted him in the midst of the Philistines who ruled over Israel. God was going to use Samson to bring judgment on the Philistines because they possessed the Ark of the LORD and were oppressing Israel. Samson was a judge over the Children of Israel, chosen by God. The form of judgment that God was going to show was the destruction of many by one. The life of Samson is a testimony of how God can use one willing vessel to demonstrate His supreme power to thousands and to other nations. Samson was anointed by God with supernatural strength. With this strength Samson killed a lion with his hands; he killed a thousand Philistines with the jaw bone of an ass and destroyed the temple of Dagon, killing himself and the host of Philistines who had come to worship Dagon.

Samson's strength was from God. The gift of strength was symbolized and sealed by the physical restrictions that had been placed on Samson. These physical conditions were the evidence of Samson's service and submission to God. He was not to drink strong drink nor to cut his hair. To drink or to cut his hair would be an act of rebellion and sin. By doing this he would remove himself from the blessings of God.

Judgment, however, fell on Samson. Delilah had tempted him over and over to reveal the secret of his strength. Although he had lied to her in the past, this time he told the truth. Delilah had his hair cut off and thus delivered him to the Philistines. The strength of God left him since his vows as a Nazarite had been violated by the cutting of his hair. The promise was broken; Samson had disobeyed God. The Philistines, by cutting off Samson's hair, rendered Samson harmless. They put out his eyes and cast him into the dungeons of the temple of Dagon.

When God provides us with the strength to accomplish his works, or when He gives us a provision or miracle of grace, we must keep the conditions He demands of us. Let us not break covenant with God and take for granted His provision; to do so is to bring our own ruin.

God's grace, however, is not dependant on us. Samson's hair grew back. One day the Philistines had a great celebration and decided to make sport of Samson. They brought him up and placed him among the pillars of the temple of Dagon. *"Samson said to the servant who held his hand, 'Put me where I can feel the pillars that support the temple, so that I may lean against them.' Now the temple was crowded with men and women; all the rulers of the Philistines were there, and on the roof were about three thousand men and women watching Samson perform. Then Samson prayed to the Lord, 'O Sovereign Lord, remember me. O God, please strengthen me just once more, and let me with one blow get revenge on the Philistines for my two eyes.' Then Samson reached toward the two central pillars on which the temple stood. Bracing himself against them, his right hand on the one and his left hand on the other,*

Samson said, 'Let me die with the Philistines!' Then he pushed with all his might, and down came the temple on the rulers and all the people in it. Thus he killed many more when he died than while he lived" (Judg. 16:26-30).

The Fiery Furnace

When we follow the will of the Lord instead of the will of man, fire shall not burn us when it falls on us, neither shall poisonous snakes harm us when they bite us. Although the king of Babylon had commanded all to bow down to his image, Shadrach, Meshach and Abednego served God and would bow to no man. The king was furious and had them thrown into a furnace to be burnt alive. But when he looked into the furnace to watch their death, he saw a fourth image with them in the fire (Jesus!). They were walking around, not at all bothered by the flames! The king had them removed and examined the three (the fourth had vanished). They didn't even smell of smoke, nor was their hair singed by the extreme heat. God had protected them.

We have a similar promise: *"Fear not, for I have redeemed you; I have called you by name; you are mine. When you pass through the waters, I will be with you; and when you pass through the rivers, they will not sweep over you. When you walk through the fire, you will not be burned; the flames will not set you ablaze. For I am the Lord, your God, the Holy One of Israel, your Savior..."* (Isa. 43:1-3). Fire is symbolic of trials and temptation. Those who walk with Christ cannot be hurt or overcome by them. This is the spiritual interpretation of the scriptures, obviously there was, and is, a natural one as well.

When Paul was shipwrecked on the island of Malta, he was bitten by a poisonous snake. The islanders thought he would be dead within minutes; he wasn't. In fact, he showed no side effects at all. God protected His servant (Acts 28:1-6). Jesus promises that His disciples are protected by Him: *"they will pick up snakes with their hands; and when they drink deadly poison, it will not hurt them at all; they will place their hands on sick people, and they will get well"* (Mark 16:18). This is the promise of God.

The miracles that happen physically to the believer are many. There are numerous healings recorded throughout the scriptures: sight restored, the lame walk, and even the dead arise at God's command. The clothes of the Children of Israel actually grew on them in the wilderness...Enoch walked right into heaven...Lazarus was raised from the dead...the skills of David were increased to kill the enemy of the Lord. The list goes on.

For those who come against the Lord there is both physical and spiritual judgment. The Philistines were destroyed by Samson. When Miriam challenged God's will to have Moses as the leader, she was struck with leprosy (Num. 12). When the Children of Israel danced sinfully before an idol, they had to drink the gold from that idol and many died (Ex. 32). Lot's wife was turned to salt when she disobeyed God by looking back on Sodom and Gomorrah (Gen. 19). Pharoah and Egypt were visited by plagues because they would not release the Hebrews (Ex. 7-11). When Zechariah didn't believe what God said, he was made dumb until the word of the Lord was fulfilled (Luke 1). Not trusting and walking with God brings sickness and death, just as trusting Him brings life. The reason for this is that God is the Source of health and life. When we believe on Him we have health and life; when we don't believe we lose them.

There is an example of the danger of taking for granted the acts of the Lord and misusing His blessings to us. The Lord's Supper is a communion between God and us; it is a reminder of Jesus' sacrifice on the cross, His life given for the remission of our sins. When we partake of communion we are declaring our fellowship with the cross —that we are crucified with Jesus to rise in new life. If someone knows Jesus and participates in communion with mockery or irreverence, the result is sickness or even death. In the outpouring of His blood and the breaking of His body, Christ took on all sickness and paid for death to be abolished; thus we have health and life. When we reject or mock this provision, we expose ourselves to the possibility of sickness and death. When one rejects the blood and body of Christ, the same will bear the cost of sin which is sickness and death. For these reasons Paul writes... *"Therefore, whoever eats the bread or drinks of the cup of the Lord in an unworthy manner will be guilty of sinning against the body and blood of the Lord. A man ought to examine himself before he eats of the bread and drinks of the cup. For anyone who eats and drinks without recognizing the body of the Lord eats and drinks judgment on himself. That is why many among you are weak and sick, and a number of you have fallen asleep"* (I Cor. 11:27-30).

Let us all look toward Christ and ask for His light to shine through us, as we lift our eyes to behold our King. Let our arms be uplifted in victorious praise, as we rejoice in the strength of the Lord's deliverance. In all things, let us look forward to the health and life which Christ purchased for us on the cross. In all our actions may we remember the Lord with reverence.

MAN TO GOD

TRUE AND FALSE

1. T F God's power is sometimes seen in the physical body of a person.

2. T F The face is the second most communicative part of the body.

3. T F A person's face can actually shine with the joy of God.

4. T F The eyes reflect life and emotion.

5. T F As long as Aaron and Joshua held up the hands of Moses they won the battle.

6. T F God can renew your physical strength.

7. T F Samson was blind when he killed the greatest number of Philistines.

8. T F   Jesus was in the furnace with Shadrach, Meshach and Abednego.

9. T F   Jesus promised we would not be hurt by poison when in His service.

10. T F   We are not changed physically by the presence of the Lord.

GROUP DISCUSSION

1. What physical miracles have we seen? What are some of the ways we see Jesus in other people?

2. Why did God allow Job to go through the physical hardships he went through?

3. What are some of the promises God has for us physically?

PERSONAL ASSIGNMENT

1. Rewrite man's involvement at the crucifixion of Jesus. Note the effect it has on the living and the dead.

2. Make a list of the gestures which God commands us to use, i.e. praise His name in the dance, clap our hands, etc.

ANSWERS TO THE TRUE AND FALSE

1. T, 2. F, 3. T, 4. T, 5. F, 6. T, 7. T, 8. T, 9. T, 10. F

Chapter V

DANCE AND PRAISE

Let them praise his name in the dance (Ps. 149:3 KJV).

We are commanded to praise God with the dance. Scripturally, one cannot argue this point. The point of discussion is how, when, where and why. What form shall it take and who is to dance? These and other questions must be answered before we re-establish dance. If dance is to be restored to the church, it must have a firm foundation or it will fall into destruction and be cast aside. We have seen, in the past, where dance has been raised up only to fall in disarray. We must set up that foundation, for the answers we find will be the building ground for the future.

In order for us to understand the use of dance today we must understand its use in scripture. God's Word gives us clear guidelines to follow for the dance. We must not limit our interpretation to the present-day understanding of dance — dance as an art form and a courting-coupling activity. This understanding is too limited and does not reflect dance as seen in scripture. We must put aside our viewpoints, perspectives and cultural prejudice and open our hearts to understanding as found through the study of God's Word and the inspiration of the Holy Spirit.

THE HEBREWS AND DANCE

Dance to the Hebrew was an expression of life and religious service. Dance was the physical demonstration of the interior emotion, the expression of joy, the activity birthed by joy.

...a time to mourn, and a time to dance...(Eccl. 3:4).

You turned my wailing into dancing; (Ps. 30:11).

Joy is gone from our hearts; our dancing has turned to mourning (Lam. 5:15).

Dance is clearly seen as an expression of the joy of life. The scriptural opposite of mourning and sorrow is dancing (which is of joy). When dancing is taken away we have mourning.

The Hebrews viewed life as a complete unit; they did not divide it into unrelated parts. Their spiritual life was as important as their physical life; the spiritual was actually part of the physical.

As a result of this view, dance was used for both religious and (as we would say) non-religious events. Life to the

Hebrews was an expression of their religion. Dance, however, can be seen from three different points of focus:

1. Man to man — cultural expression
2. Man to God — praise/worship and prayer
3. God to man — ministry — prophecy

At times these points of focus overlapped. The Hebrew people frequently experienced the spiritual in the midst of their everyday, natural existence.

The Appearances of the Word 'Dance'

The word dance appears 27 times in the Bible. Though the use of the word 'dance' is found a limited amount of times, the activity of dancing is not so limited. It actually appears hundreds of times throughout the Old and New Testaments. This can be seen in the verb roots of many Hebrew and Greek words. Many words actually include dance activity in their meanings. These words include: rejoice, glad, exceedingly glad, exalt, make merry, exceeding joy, joy, players (musicians) on instruments, play, rejoiced greatly, praise, celebrate, feasts (Passover, First Fruits — harvest — Tabernacles) and bless. Remember when you read these words that their expression often includes dance movements or dance itself!

Let us be glad [as a lamb skipping and frolicking for joy] *and rejoice,* [leap and skip for joy], *and give honour to him: for the marriage of the Lamb is come, and his wife hath made herself ready* (Rev. 19:7 KJV).

Your father Abraham rejoiced [leaped forward with joy] *at the thought of seeing my day; he saw it and was **glad*** (John 8:56, author's emphasis).

The singers went before, the players on instruments [musicians who also dance in a processional] *followed after; among them were the damsels **playing with timbrels*** (Ps. 68:25 KJV, author's emphasis).

In many versions "players on instruments" is translated into the word "musicians." However, it is important to note that these musicians were not seated; they were dancing, playing and moving to the "rhythm of their music." They were "***players** on instruments.*" Almost any museum has painted bowls and vases of the ancients, which depict the figure of a double-pipe player dancing to his own tune.

TYPES OF DANCES

Dances of Courtship

Two references stand out from the Biblical examples of courtship dancing, these being Judges 21:21 and Song of Solomon 6:13.

Judges 20 and 21 tell the story of the Benjamites going to war against Israel (their brothers) and being defeated. During the war they lose their wives to fire. Israel had sworn not to give them wives, so even after the war was over they couldn't help the Benjamites. The tribe found some wives among the people of Jabesh Gilead. The elders of Israel desired that the Benjamite tribe be preserved and restored to fellowship. So, the elders counseled the Benjamites to go to the feast held at Shiloh (the Feast of Tabernacles), to wait for the daughters of Shiloh to dance in the vineyard (during the Days of Atonement), to hide themselves in the vineyard and capture the girls as they passed by, and then to take them home and marry them. This story sounds rather bizarre. One could feel sorry for the women who had to marry into such a troublesome tribe. However, there is more to the story.

According to Jewish Rabbis, this scripture makes reference to a coupling dance which took place at the time of the Feast of Tabernacles, during the Days of Atonement. The women were said to exchange dresses with each other, so no one would be ashamed if she didn't have a suitable dress. Then the women would go out into the vineyards and call to the available men to come and choose a bride from among them. "The beautiful among them called out, 'set your eyes on beauty, for the quality most prized in woman is beauty.' Those of them who came of noble families called out, 'look for [a good] family, for woman has been created to bring up a family.' The ugly ones among them called out 'carry off your purchase in the name of Heaven, only on one condition, that you adorn us with jewels of gold' " (The Talmud).

According to my references, this was a yearly event, not just a one-time occasion. The apparent reason for its existence was to permit intermarriage among tribes and classes. Though the Feast of Tabernacles existed during both the good and evil years of Israel, this cultural custom is assumed by many to be the result of the evil days of Israel's history. Nowhere else are courting dances mentioned in scripture (though outside resources say they existed during these times). One must question if this courting dance is the result of Judges 21:25, which immediately follows the story of the Benjamites seeking wives: *"In those days Israel had no King; everyone did as he saw fit."* In the King James, this time period is referred to as the time when *"every man did that which was right in his own eyes."*

What is the purpose and benefit of the 'courting dances' of today? Are we to marry the one we dance with or are we just stirring the flesh?

The Marriage Dance

Dancing at weddings was common among the Hebrews. In Revelation 19:7 the bride of Christ is seen as rejoicing (leaping). In Song of Solomon 6:13 the Shulamite (symbol of the Bride of Christ) makes reference to the 'dance of two armies' or 'the dance of Mahanaim." It has been said that this dance was one of the following:

1. a processional of the bride; or
2. a dance which was done by the bridegroom with a sword to symbolically fend off any who would try to take the bride.

Whatever the case, it was a marriage dance. The idea of a husband and wife dancing together is well supported.

Victory Dances

Victory dances were done to celebrate. Many of them included a processional.

Victory dance toward man are present in the Bible (Judg. 11:34; I Sam. 18:6; 21:11; 29:5). Although man's receiving praise through dance is not directly condemned, we do see that negative things take place whenever man is glorified. The sacrifice of a virgin's life follows the victory dance described in Judges 11:34. The result of the victory dance given to David in I Samuel 18:6 is the jealousy of Saul and the suspicion of the Philistines.

Victory dances (dance troupes) toward God are also recorded in the Bible. Exodus 15 describes the victory celebration commemorating the salvation of Israel by the drowning of the army of Egypt in the Red Sea and Israel's safe passage through that sea. The dances seen here are led by the prophetess Miriam. She came forth playing a tambourine followed by all the women who were playing tambourines and dancing (Ex. 15:20). The dance was done while sections of the Song of Moses were repeated (Ex. 15:20). It has been said that this was a spontaneous dance. Many reject this theory since the original meaning of the word suggests a more developed dance which might have depicted the victory of God in mime-dance. The theory of a more developed dance is also supported by the well-structured form of the Song of Moses, the possi-bility of a time for preparation before the Song of Moses was sung and danced, and the common cultural practice to celebrate with pre-choreographed movement.

Whatever the case, the important thing to note is that we can praise God through the use of a troupe of dancers (be the dance spontaneous or choreographed) while others continue to praise God by singing along. This dance is under the direction of one chosen by God (as in the case of the *prophetess* Miriam); it is not just one person, or a group of people, "doing their own thing." It is a dance which fits in and flows with the general direction of the praise being led by a spiritual leader (be it Moses, the pastor, or a worship leader).

GROUP DANCES

Processionals

There are many processionals mentioned or alluded to in scripture. These include the ones mentioned as victory dances (Judg. 11:34). Processionals were also used to usher in royalty, both earthly and heavenly (I Sam. 18:6; Matt. 21:4-11). They were used to welcome or transport an important personage. Processionals were used by priests in the offering of sacrifices and the services at the altar (Ps. 47:5; I Kings 18:32-40). Processions were included in expressions of praise and worship (Ps. 47; 48:12-14; 95:1-2; 100:2-4; 118:19-29; 132:8-10; 149; 150).

The most noted processional of the Bible is the processional which brought the Ark of the Covenant to Zion

(II Sam. 6:1-5,12-16; I Chron. 15:25-29). King David
and all of Israel is seen bringing the Ark back to Jerusalem
with singing, dancing (playing), leaping and the playing
of instruments.

> *David and the whole house of Israel were celebra-
> ting* [dancing] *with all their might before the Lord,
> with songs and with harps, lyres, tambourines, sistrums
> and cymbals* (II Sam. 6:5).

May we likewise usher in the presence of the Lord into
our Zion, that He might reign and dwell with us!

An example of the idolatrous use of the processional is
seen in the contest between the prophets of Baal and the
prophet Elijah (I Kings 18:21-40). The priests of Baal are
pictured holding a processional around the altars of sacrifice, calling upon their god as they leaped and hopped on
and around their altar. The dances of the priests of Baal
were accompanied by cutting the flesh and crying out.
Elijah mocked them for their vain gestures as they tried
to awaken Baal, and proceeded to show forth the power
of God. The result of the sin of the priests of Baal was
shame and death. It was not the hopping and leaping that
was wrong, it was the use of it to worship a false god.
How many people today worship a false god, the god of
flesh and man, through the vain dances of today? What is
the result of such dances?

Dances of Restoration

Whenever the Lord brings restoration to His people

and joy is restored to the hearts of His children, dance is seen. Restoration births dance.

> *I will build you up again and you will be rebuilt, O Virgin Israel. Again you will take up your tambourines and go out to dance with the joyful* (Jer. 31:4).

> *You turned my wailing into dancing; you removed my sackcloth and clothed me with joy...*(Ps. 30:11).

In these times of restoration it is no wonder that God brings forth the dance and restores it to His people as the expression of joy and life that it was always meant to be. For those who reject God and come under His judgment, there is only sorrow without dance.

> *Joy is gone from our hearts; our dancing has turned to mourning* (Lam. 5:15).

Dances for Reunion

The story of the prodigal son illustrates the use of dance to celebrate the homecoming of a lost son. It is a parable told by Jesus (Luke 15:11-31). Jesus used the natural event of a homecoming to express the spiritual event of a homecoming. The Hebrew people would rejoice with song and dance when a lost member of the family returned. In heaven, all the angels dance at the salvation of each person, rejoicing at his or her return to the family of God.

Dances of Praise

All of the children of God are commanded to dance

before the Lord, both as a group and as individuals. This means dance in general, not just a refined dance. Indeed it might include leaping, skipping, hopping or the "charismatic four-step," as well as the developed dance.

> *Let Israel rejoice in their Maker; let the people of Zion be glad in their King. Let them praise his name with dancing...*(Ps. 149:2-3).

> *...praise him with tambourine and dancing...*(Ps. 150:4).

Idolatrous Dance

In Exodus 32, the Israelites got tired of waiting for Moses to come down from Mount Sinai where he was receiving instruction from the Lord. They decided to make their own god from the gold they had brought up out of Egypt. After they made this idol, a golden calf, they sacrificed to it and *"sat down to eat and drink and got up to indulge in revelry"* (Ex. 32:6b). According to the Hebrew word "revelry," this passage suggests sexual play. In the worship of false gods, suggestive dance and sexual acts were often a part of the religious celebration. The Canaanites believed this would persuade the gods to grant fertility to the people, their flocks and their souls. The Israelites probably brought some of this thought with them from their life in Egypt.

The result of the idolatry of Israel was the wrath of God. They suffered humiliation, physical discomfort (having to drink the ground-down gold of the calf, which doesn't pass through the system with grace!), a plague and death (Ex. 32-33).

Now these things occurred as examples, to keep us from setting our hearts on evil things as they did. Do not be idolaters, as some of them were; as it is written: "The people sat down to eat and drink and got up to indulge in pagan revelry." We should not commit sexual immorality, as some of them did — and in one day twenty-three thousand died... These things happened to them as examples and were written down as warnings for us...(I Cor. 10:6-11).

Let us beware not to dance in a manner which is sexually suggestive and provocative, like much of the "coupling-dance" of our society! We have been warned.

SOLO DANCES

There are two outstanding solo dances in the Old and New Testaments. These are the dance of Salome and the dance of David. Salome's dance was done unto man; David's dance was done unto God.

The Dance of Salome

King Herod had married his brother's wife, Herodias. John the Baptist spoke against this and was arrested and put in prison. Although Herodias wanted John dead, King Herod feared to kill him. During a banquet, Salome, the daughter of Herodias, danced for Herod. It is believed that the dance was a form of "Roman Pantomimus" which was a sensual dance form common to those days. It so pleased Herod that he promised Salome anything she wished. Following the prompting of her mother, Salome asked for the head of John the Baptist. Herod felt honor bound before his guests and had John beheaded (Matt. 14:6; Mark 6:22). Salome's dance glorified man's flesh and resulted in death. Dance which manipulates and provokes the flesh is sinful. The attention of Salome's dance was toward herself; there was no place for God.

The Dance of David

This is probably the most quoted scriptural reference to dance. The scripture tells us about the return of the Ark of the Testimony to the Children of Israel, after its long absence. David and all the Children of Israel brought it to Zion in a grand processional with music and joyous celebration expressed by dancing. As the Ark of the Lord approached Zion, King David took off his kingly robes and danced before the procession of the Ark of Witness in the linen ephod worn only by the priests. He danced and led the people to the resting ground for the Ark of the Covenant (II Sam. 6:14; I Chron. 15:29).

It is important to note that scripture states that David was "dancing before the Lord" and not "dancing in the spirit." (This term never appears in scripture).

David, wearing a linen ephod, danced before the Lord with all his might, while he and the entire house of Israel brought up the ark of the Lord with shouts and the sound of trumpets (II Sam. 6:14-15).

It was a decision of the will for David to dance before the Lord. The Spirit of God did not take over; that would be God praising God, thus defeating the whole purpose of man's offering up his praise. God might inspire us and help us to plan, but we are the instruments of will, submitting to His Will. David's dance was planned, evident in the fact that David was already wearing the linen ephod that only Levite priests wore. David was neither Levite nor priest. David willingly put aside his pride as king and took on the role of a servant of God. His attitude shows us how to approach dance and its relationship to the body of Christ (Israel).

The differences between the dances of Salome and that of David are many. Salome danced for herself and the pleasure of man. David danced as king, representing the people of Israel before God, and as priest (in linen ephod), praising God in the dance. His dance was for God's pleasure. The result of Salome's dance was death. The result of David's dance was the expression of life. Salome expressed sin; David expressed joy. The dance of Salome is an example of that which should not be done; the dance of David is an example of that which should be done.

DANCE FORMS

There is no form of dance which is higher than another; Israeli folk dance is no better than ballet or jazz. Although some dance forms lend themselves easier to the expression of worship, all forms can be used. We must be careful with gestures and make certain they communicate godly thought and not lust. It is most important that the dance clearly communicates a thought or a feeling. The purpose of dance is to communicate the joy of life, not to bring confusion and disorder.

The actual form of Hebrew dance is not seen today. God's purpose for this loss might be to show us that it is never the gesture that is important. What is important is that which a gesture communicates. A jump is a jump, be it in ballet, jazz or folk dance; what the jump communicates is the important point.

CRITICS BEWARE!

We must be careful not to judge the dances of praise given by the pure in heart.

As the ark of the Lord was entering the City of David, Michal daughter of Saul watched from a window. And when she saw King David leaping and dancing before the Lord, she despised him in her heart.... When David returned home to bless his household, Michal daughter of Saul came out to meet him and said, "How the king of Israel has distinguished himself today, disrobing in the sight of the slave girls of his servants as any vulgar fellow would!" David said to Michal, "It was before the Lord, who chose me rather than your father or anyone from his house when he appointed me ruler over the Lord's people Israel — I will celebrate [dance] *before the Lord. I will become even more undignified than this, and I will be humiliated in my own eyes. But by these slave girls you spoke of, I will be held in honour." And Michal daughter of Saul **had no children** to the day of her death* (II Sam. 6:16,20-23, author's emphasis).

Michal's focus was on position and pride, David's on servanthood and humbleness before God. Michal was concerned about the people's response; David was concerned about God's response. He knew that by glorifying God he would be honoured. Michal was of the old order of Israel (Saul); David was of the new order of Israel under God. David's spirit praised God; Michal was barren.

DANCE

TRUE AND FALSE

1. T   F   We are not commanded to praise God in the dance.

2. T   F   Dance is the exterior expression of interior joy.

3. T   F   The term "players on instruments" refers to musicians who danced and moved to the rhythm of their music.

4. T   F   There was a courting dance mentioned in Judges that took place during the Feast of Passover.

5. T F The victory dance given in honour of David and Saul resulted in jealousy and suspicion.

6. T F Processionals of the Bible were sometimes joyous events having loud praises, shouts and dancing to music.

7. T F David "danced in the spirit" with all his might.

8. T F Israeli folk dance is the scriptural dance of David.

GROUP DISCUSSION

1. What governs the expression of dance when it is done by the whole church, a troupe, a soloist?

2. When is dancing wrong or right?

3. If we believe that these are the days of restoration, does this mean that God is going to restore the dance and arts to the Church? If so how will this take place? What must we do?

4. Some people find it easier to accept cultural dancing than praise dance. Why? What does scripture say?

PERSONAL ASSIGNMENT

1. List and study the actual appearance of dance in scripture.

2. Do a study of the related words of dance: i.e. rejoice, joy, etc.

3. Write down your thoughts about dance and its purpose in society as an expression; then compare it to scripture.

ANSWERS TO THE TRUE AND FALSE

1.F, 2.T, 3.T, 4.F, 5.T, 6.T, 7.T, 8.F

Chapter VI

PROPHETIC DRAMA
AND JEWISH MIME

I have also spoken [to you] *by the prophets and I
have multiplied visions* [for you] *and* [have appealed
to you] *through parables acted out by the prophets*
(Hos. 12:10 Amp.).

Throughout scripture, God has used dramatic expression to communicate His Will and His Word. This might
be in Jewish mime, acting, storytelling, parable, allegory,
song, dance, gestural communication, sign, etc. God's
Word is full of examples of the ministering arts and the
fine arts. However, we have failed to see what is obviously
there. Why? Simply because we read the Bible, instead of
seeing it. We read what they enacted. There are numerous
examples of the arts in prophecy. Mime is used over 40
times in Scripture. Over one-third of the ministry of

Ezekiel is done in Jewish mime. Parables, as a form of storytelling, are used over 49 times. A majority of these were spoken by Jesus. Parable, in a general sense, is seen over 250 times throughout the Old and New Testaments. The Song of Solomon is a narrative allegory. The whole life of Hosea was a living prophetic drama. These are but a few examples.

Hosea 12:10 brings out many important points about the arts:

1. God chooses to speak to us through the use of the arts.

2. The artist is a minister of God, separated unto God and under the direction of God.

3. The ministry of the arts is a prophetic call.

If we can understand the dramas and arts that took place in scripture in a living, dramatic way, we will gain a richer comprehension of God's Word, and therefore, of God.

JEWISH MIME

Jewish mime is seen when a prophet uses gestures and movements to communicate his message. These "mimes" are delivered in three ways:

1. Actions with no narrative,
2. Actions with narrative before or after,
3. Actions with narrative given at the same time.

Eighty percent of communication is non-verbal. This makes the message delivered with mime powerfully clear and very well communicated. Those who would no longer hear the Word of the Lord...could see it.

The eight messengers who stand out in their use of mime are: Agabus, Ahijah, Angel in Revelation, Elisha, Ezekiel, Hosea, Isaiah and Jeremiah.

Mime is used to show God's judgment (I Kings 11:30-40), to show God's provisional will (II Kings 13:15-19), to illustrate judgments of shame (Isa. 20:1-6), to foretell and warn (as seen in the prophesies of Ezekiel and Jeremiah*), and to make clear the results of one's actions (Acts 21:10-11). The list can go on. Let us sum it up by stating that mime is used to clarify, illustrate and demonstrate.

Ezekiel's Mimes

In 597 B.C., Nebuchadnezzar attacked Jerusalem, plundered the city and deported the King, Jehoiachin, and many others to Babylon. Ezekiel was deported at this time and took residence at Tel-abib, beside the river, Chebar, along with the majority of the exiled ones. While in captivity, Ezekiel received his commission from Yahweh, at the age of 30. He ministered through Jewish

---

*Jewish mime of Jeremiah and Ezekiel: Jer. 13:1-4,18,19; 25:15-38; 27:1-28; 43:8-13; 51:62-64; Ezek. 3:26-27; 4:1-17; 5:1-17; 6:1-14; 7:23-27; 12:1-6; 17-28; 20:45-49; 21:1-7,12-23; 24:12-23; 32:17-21; 37:1-25.

mime, speech, acting, visions, symbols, allegories and parables.

The prophet Ezekiel was not able to speak; he had to mime his prophecy unless he prophesied with a "Thus saith the Lord."

I will make your tongue stick to the roof of your mouth so that you will be silenced and unable to rebuke them [Israel], though they are a rebellious house. But when I speak to you, I will open your mouth and you shall say to them, "This is what the Sovereign Lord says." Whoever will listen let him listen, and whoever will refuse let him refuse; for they are a rebellious house (Ezek. 3:26-27).

Read Ezekiel, chapters 4 to 6. Note the prophesies in which no speaking was involved; many of the prophesies are just acted out. Re-read chapter 4, verses 1 to 3. In these verses, Ezekiel is commanded to enact the capture and defeat of Jerusalem. He is to do so in silence. He first draws the city of Jerusalem on a brick and sets this brick in front of him. Then he shows the different stages of attack that the city will go through (by attacking the brick). After showing the siege of the city, he then shows that there is a barrier between the city and God (seen by the use of the iron pan). *It is possible this barrier was created by the rebellious sins of Israel.* This barrier stopped God from helping them; because of it, they could not get through to God with pleas for help. This prophecy is fulfilled in II Kings 23:28-25:30 and II Chronicles 35:20-36:23.

The people of Israel would not listen to the Word of the Lord. False prophets were declaring a word contrary to the Word of the Lord as spoken by the true prophets of God. The people chose to listen to the false prophets' word. They did not heed the Word of the Lord because the false prophesy was easier to enfold and the Children of Israel were a rebellious people. Because the Children of Israel would no longer listen to the Word of God, God had His prophets show His word in mime! Now the people would see what they wouldn't hear. Both Ezekiel and Jeremiah used this form to reach a closed-eared people. Mime showed to people what they wouldn't hear.

DRAMA

The Drama of Hosea

The whole life and ministry of Hosea has been referred to as a living drama. All the events of his life had symbolic meaning for the Children of Israel. The book of Hosea is noted for its figures of speech: parables, metaphors, figurative illustrations and parabolic sentences. One writer speaks of Hosea saying "the language of the prophet resembles a garland of divers flowers; images are woven to images, similes strung to similes, metaphors ranged on metaphors."

Hosea lived in the days of King Jeroboam II, ministering at the same time as Isaiah and Amos. Israel, during this time, was showing herself to be unfaithful to Jehovah. She was unfaithful in political alliances and in idolatry. Israel shunned God's love and turned to a life of sin.

Hosea is told to marry Gomer, an adulterous woman (many believe her unfaithfulness occurred after the marriage). This was to illustrate the way God's people, Israel, had shown themselves to be unfaithful to God by worshipping Baal and persisting in lawlessness. After a time of separation and judgment because of Gomer's (Israel) actions, Gomer is restored to the unquenchable love and devotion of Hosea (God). Hosea is a book which speaks of the unfailing love of God even when His children have strayed and sinned against Him. Even though they brought judgment upon themselves, God is faithful to forgive and bring restoration.

The symbols of Hosea are many. Some of them are as follows:

The adulteress Gomer...the idolatry of Israel
The Children of Gomer...the Lord's judgments
   Jezreel...the punishment to come
   Lo-Ruhamah...without compassion or love
   Lo-Ammi...not my people
Gomer in the Wilderness...the separation of Israel from
   God
The whirlwind...the judgments of God
Gomer restored to Hosea...Israel to be restored to God
Lo-Ruhamah becomes Ruhamah...the love of God
   given
Lo-Ammi becomes Ammi...the people of God
Being planted...firmly established in God

I will plant her for myself in the land; I will show my love to the one I called "Not my loved one." I will say to those called "Not my people," "You are my people"; and they will say, "You are my God." (Hos. 2:23).

Use a commentary and study the metaphors found in Hosea 14 in which the beauty of the restored Children of God is pictured as a lily that grows quickly and is beautiful; an olive tree, renowned for its manifold uses; a cedar of Lebanon, full of fragrance (which is symbolic of the fragrance and strength of a life lived in the will of God). Continue on your own.

Drama is used to reveal the ways of God in a natural analogy and to express life in its found state of being.

PARABLE

For since the creation of the world God's invisible qualities — his eternal power and divine nature — have been clearly seen, being understood from what has been made...(Rom. 1:20).

A parable uses the objects of God's visible creation to teach us truths about His invisible and spiritual kingdom.

The parable was frequently and commonly used by the ancients (Greeks, Romans, Hebrews, etc.) as a tool for teaching morals and spiritual truths. A parable commonly consisted of some form of a short story where the truths and meanings were hidden inside the fictitious account of an event or object. Generally the account was feasible and involved a topic that was understood by all: planting a field, shipping, losing a son. It was during the interpretation of these events that the moral or spiritual truth was found.

> *The disciples came to him* [Jesus] *and asked, "Why do you speak to the people in parables?"*
>
> *He replied, "The knowledge of the secrets of the kingdom of heaven has been given to you, but not to them. Whoever has will be given more, and he will have an abundance. Whoever does not have, even what he has will be taken from him. This is why I speak to them in parables: 'Though seeing, they do not see; though hearing, they do not hear or understand.'"*
> (Matt. 13:11-13).

Parables reveal truth to teach each person as he is ready to receive it — each to his own measure. Those who are not open to the truths of God will not see the truths revealed in the parable. Parables explain the mysteries of God by comparing them to the natural world which we know and understand.

Jesus' use of parable fulfilled the prophecy of Isaiah (Matt. 13:14). Jesus' parables are considered the most developed and richly symbolic of all parables; they are masterpieces without compare.

The parables of Jesus illustrated faith (Luke 13:18-19; Mark 4:30-32), the joy of heaven when one is saved (Luke 15:11-32), and God's love for each of us (Matt. 18:10-14); they also teach the things of the kingdom (Matt. 7; 9; 13; 14; 18; 21; 22; Mark 2; 4; 12; 13; Luke 6; 7; 8; 10; 11; 12; 13; 15; 17; 18; 19; 21).

The Parable of Dogs, Pigs and Pearls

Many of the parables of Jesus are well-known and frequently studied. Although this parable is one of the shorter ones, it is still full of meaning.

Do not give dogs what is sacred; do not throw your pearls to pigs. If you do, they may trample them under their feet, and then turn and tear you to pieces (Matt. 7:6).

In order to understand this parable, let's cross reference it with other reference to dogs, pigs and pearls.

Watch out for those dogs, those men who do evil, those mutilators of the flesh (Phil. 3:2).

There are people who have known righteousness and tasted of the life with Christ. Some of them, after knowing the way of righteousness, turn their backs on God and fall back into a state of sin and worldly ways; they return to their old nature. *"Of them the proverbs are true: 'A dog returns to its vomit,' and, 'A sow that is washed goes back to her wallowing in the mud' "* (II Pet. 2:22).

Outside are the dogs, those who practice magic arts, the sexually immoral, the murderers, the idolaters and everyone who loves and practices falsehood (Rev. 22:15).

Again, the kingdom of heaven is like a merchant looking for fine pearls. When he found one of great value, he went away and sold everything he had and bought it (Matt. 13:45).

Dogs and pigs represent those who profess to be Christians but do not possess Christ. Their belief is merely an intellectual assent.

The dog is the one who, when he hears about God, leaves a life of sin for a time, only to return to it later (as a dog returning to his own vomit). He is violent in his sin and destroys other people by involving them in his sin. If you associate with him, he will drag you into his life of sin and lead you astray. As the King James Version reads "Beware of Dogs!"

The pig is the one who has only changed exteriorly, reforming the outward appearance. The inward man is still full of sin. He is not renewed in Christ nor is he born again. He is impure and unclean (Mosaic law). His impurity will be revealed. Exterior change will last for only a brief period before there is evidence of the true self. "A pig may be washed, but its unclean nature still remains" (Zodhiates). It will return to the mud. The person who changes only on the outside will return to sin.

Pearls speak of things of great value. In this case they refer to the truths of the Kingdom of God.

Dogs and pigs are not worthy of these treasures. They will only throw them away, abusing the truth or causing the giver damage. We should not try to teach the deep things of God to people who have chosen to reject God after knowing Him. It's dangerous for us to associate with them. They will not appreciate or accept the truth —

they will try to destroy it. For this reason, among others, Jesus used parables.

The Parable of Nathan

The parable Nathan told to King David (II Sam. 11-12, 12:1-4) is one of the more well-known and more potent parables of the Old Testament. II Samuel 11 tells the story how King David, when he was home from war, saw Bathsheba bathing and lusted after her. He then called her to his room and sinned; she conceived. At this point David tried to cover up his sin by calling her husband home from war, with the hope that her husband would sleep with Bathsheba. However, much to David's demise, Uriah (Bathsheba's husband) would not return home and could not be tricked into going home (though David tried). Uriah was commited to share the conditions of the men of Israel and God's Ark. Since they couldn't return home, neither would he. David figured then that the only way to solve the problem was to kill Uriah and marry Bathsheba, thus fulfilling his lust. When he sent Uriah back to war, Uriah carried a letter to Joab from King David. In it David commanded Joab to place Uriah at the front of the battle and leave him there to be killed by the enemy. Uriah never knew that he carried his own death warrant. Uriah was killed and David married Bathsheba. David's heart had become calloused and hard. This act as well as David's response to the loss of a battle and the death of Uriah reflect his hardness of heart.

David told the messenger, "Say this to Joab: 'Don't
let this upset you; the sword devours one as well as
another. Press the attack against the city and destroy
it.' Say this to encourage Joab" (II Sam. 11:25).

At this point David's heart is hard and most believe
that he would have been closed to an open rebuke for his
sin. Truly, how could you prove that he had sinned? If
someone had come to him with an accusation, he probably
would have said "prove it." He, like many of us, had
walls of defense through which no words could break.
God had a way.

Nathan may have known about David's sin before
going to visit him, but he waited. Then *"the Lord sent*
Nathan to David" (II Sam. 12:1). Nathan spoke not a
word of rebuke to David; he simply told him a parable.
The parable stirred the emotions of David and thereby
opened his heart. Nathan totally passed David's defenses
by approaching him at the point of his sin. He did not
preach to him about the need for holiness. (We can learn
from this. How many of us approach someone who is
living in sin with a demand for holiness, instead of re-
sponding to him in the state of sin? Until THEY see their
sin, they will not see the need to be holy.) We must learn
to approach people where they are at, not where they
should be. Nathan approached David as one seeking the
advice of the king and judge of the people. He didn't
approach David with a tone of superiority, but as a
subject servant. Thus King David judged the parable of

Nathan. Read II Samuel 12:1-7. David's emotions were stirred by the parable and he became angry with the rich man who stole and killed the lamb. (Being a shepherd, he understood the value of a ewe.) He then pronounced judgment on the rich man...and thereby on himself.

Then Nathan said to David "You are the man!" (II Sam. 12:7).

David listened as Nathan drew the parallels between the characters of the parable, and Uriah and David. David saw himself as the rich man (king), Uriah as the poor man (soldier), and Bathsheba as the ewe. David, as king, had many wives (flocks and herds); Uriah had but one wife (one ewe). There was theft and murder (of the ewe and Uriah) to please desire. Nathan then pronounced the judgment of God to an open David; David repented of his sin, and God was faithful to forgive (though the consequences still existed). David in his repentance wrote the 51st Psalm. (Read it to see the complete change and attitude of the truly repentant.)

It is important to note that, as soon as David realized he was the man of the parable, he confessed. *"David said to Nathan, 'I have sinned against the Lord.' "* Nathan's reply was immediate, *"the Lord has taken away your sin, you are not going to die..."* (II Sam. 12:13).

Drama is used to go beyond the walls of man's intellect and touch the heart. Drama stirs the emotion of man and opens him up to the discipline of the Lord. Drama is used to bring repentance and salvation, by causing the individual to see his own need and to judge himself before God. Parable and drama are tools of the heart which reveal the spirit.

How do you interpret a mime, parable or drama?

1. Read the complete story in which the parable is found. Who was it written for and why? How were they affected?

2. What is the focus of the parable — to teach a truth, to bring correction, to prophecy, etc.?

3. What are the elements (the characters and events) of the parable? List them.

4. What is the natural meaning of the parable?

5. Does the scripture already interpret the parable? If so, you don't need to go much further; you run the risk of getting meanings where none are intended.

6. From your list of elements find out if and when they appear in other parts of scripture and what significance they have been given. Many times, by comparison, you'll find the possible meanings. Write them down.

7. Use a commentary to see one interpretation, and a Bible dictionary to understand the background of the people, places or events.

8. The natural meaning generally holds the key to the spiritual interpretation.

9. Divide a sheet of paper in half. On one side write the natural elements and meanings — the objects, characters, events and background. On the other side write what each of these represent (gathered from your previous work). Now reread the story by replacing the natural elements with their interpretations.

Apply these principles to the other arts.

PROPHETIC DRAMA AND JEWISH MIME

TRUE AND FALSE

1.   T   F   It is difficult to find examples of drama and art in the Bible.

2.   T   F   The ministering arts was a prophetic calling.

3.   T   F   Twenty percent of communication is verbal.

4.   T   F   The prophet Ezekiel was unable to speak, except to prophecy with a "thus saith the Lord."

5.   T   F   The life of Hosea was considered a living, dramatic prophecy.

6.   T   F   A majority of the teaching ministry of Jesus was done in parables.

7.   T   F   We should always rebuke a person living in sin with a rebuke that deals directly with the sin.

GROUP DISCUSSION

1. What natural things in our lives represent a truth, or speaks to us of a spiritual attribute?

2. How are drama and the arts used today? Is it used for the glory of God or man? How can it be brought back into an expression of the Kingdom of God?

3. If Jesus was to come back, unannounced and unrecognized by us, and started to tell us a parable, would we send Him to the Sunday School for the kids. Would the prophet Ezekiel be received? Is God going to restore all things to His people, including the arts?

PERSONAL ASSIGNMENT

1. Write your own parable and have someone else read it. Then have them tell you its meaning.

2. Analyze and interpret a parable using the method mentioned in this lesson.

ANSWERS TO THE TRUE AND FALSE

1. F, 2. T, 3. T, 4. T, 5. T, 6. T, 7. F

Chapter VII

THE FINE ARTS

In these days when God is restoring all things to their proper place, we shall see the arising of the fine arts and the ministry of the fine arts. All expressions of creativity are from God, who alone is the Creator (Gen. 1; John 1). It is by His breath and gift in us that we create and express ourselves artistically. We might misuse this gift, as many have, but the gift is still from God. How shall we use these gifts?

Each one should use whatever gift he has received to serve others, faithfully administering God's grace in various forms. If anyone speaks, he should do it as one speaking the very words of God. If anyone serves, he should do it with the strength God provides, so that in all things God may be praised through Jesus Christ. To him be the glory and the power for ever and ever. Amen (I Pet. 4:10).

THE ARTIST: BEZALEL

Bezalel was the overseeing artist for the construction of the tabernacle of Moses. We can learn many things about the life of a person called to the arts as a vocation, by studying the scriptures surrounding the work of Bezalel. Read Exodus 31:1-11; 35:30-35; and 36:1-6.

To be an artist was a vocation given by God.

Then the Lord said to Moses, "See, I have chosen Bezalel..." (Ex. 31:1-2).

This call was recognized and confirmed by leadership.

Then Moses said to the Israelites, "See, the Lord has chosen Bezalel..." (Ex. 35:30).

The artist was Spirit-filled and thus empowered to do his art.

...I [God] *have filled him with the Spirit of God* (Ex. 31:2).

He was a developed artisan, not a amateur.

I have filled him with...skill, ability and knowledge in all kinds of crafts...(Ex. 31:3).

1. Skill suggests wisdom that is based in God, who is the source of all wisdom (Job 12:13; Prov. 2:6). The Hebrew word suggests an insight and experience with all manners of art.

2. Ability suggests an understanding of the work given, discretion and insight.

3. Knowledge speaks of artistic ability that is learned by a natural process of study. It is the "know-how" of an art. God possesses all knowledge and teaches this to man (Ps. 94:10; 119:66; Prov. 2:6).

[The Hebrew word for "crafts" speaks of one's ministry, service, performance and work.]

The artist was to have an apprentice, who would help in the ministry and carry on the work.

I [God] *have appointed Oholiab...to help him* [Bezalel] (Ex. 31:6).

God has called the artist to train others in the arts so they too might glorify God in the arts. No artist is called to be the "star of the show"; he is called to reproduce the work of ministry in others.

He [God] *has given both him* [Bezalel] *and Oholiab...the ability to teach others* (Ex. 35:34).

All people who are interested in the arts should pursue their interest in the work of the Lord. However, this should be under the direction of leadership, so that the work done benefits the greater work of God.

So Bezalel, Oholiab and every skilled person to whom the Lord has given skill and ability to know how to carry out all the work of constructing the sanctuary are to do the work just as the Lord has commanded (Ex. 36:1).

All of us must remember that real knowledge comes from God (Rom. 1:18-22) and we should not be puffed up by our own knowledge (I Cor. 8:1). We should concentrate on that which is good and holy (Rom. 16:19; Phil. 4:8) and shun all appearances of evil (Eph. 5:3).

THE USES OF ART

Art can bring a person recognition with dignity and honor (Ex. 28:2,39). It can speak of the glory of the heavens, as the tabernacle is a faint copy of heaven's glory (Ex. 24:9-18; 25:40; Heb. 8:5). All things are done to glorify God. His creation shows us His truths. If we paint a waterfall, we don't have to justify the painting by putting a scripture on it (as many do). The waterfall itself is a testimony of the power and glory of God (Rom. 1:20). Art can just communicate glory, beauty and joy which are godly. However, there are uses of the arts which have brought men to repentance, salvation and a greater revelation of God.

The Brazen Serpent

The children of Israel had been wandering around the wilderness for years now, after their deliverance from Egypt. God had seen to their every need, providing water from the rock and manna to eat. Their clothes had even grown with them...yet they complained.

...they spoke against God and against Moses, and said, "Why have you brought us up out of Egypt to die in the desert? There is no bread! There is no water!

And we detest this miserable food [manna — which was savory and sweet]" (Num. 21:5).

Finally God brought a judgment on the Children of Israel:

Then the Lord sent venomous snakes among them; they bit the people and many Israelites died (Num. 21:6).

As always, Israel complained against Moses and God and then pleaded for help from the same. They were dying and if they didn't do something soon they would never see the promised land...or so they reasoned. So they went to Moses.

The people came to Moses and said, "We sinned when we spoke against the Lord and against you. Pray that the Lord will take the snakes away from us" (Num. 21:7).

The answer to the problem, according to the Israelites, was to take away the judgment God had sent... *"take the snakes away."* God had another idea. Moses went before the Lord in prayer and God gave Moses His plan.

The Lord said to Moses, "Make a snake and put it up on a pole; anyone who is bitten can look at it and live" (Num. 21:8).

And that is exactly what Moses did; and whenever the Children of Israel were bitten they would look at the bronze snake and they would be healed.

That all sounds simple enough, but upon examination it reveals great truths and the wisdom of God.

The Children of Israel had complained numerous times before and would again. When God brought the judgment of snakes upon them and they started to die off, they weren't repentant of their sin, they just didn't want to die. They were like a child who is caught with his hand in the cookie jar. He's not sorry he was trying to get a cookie. He's sorry he was caught! The Children of Israel were sorry, not that they had sinned, but that their sin had brought the snakes. This is reflected by the fact that they asked Moses to pray that *"the Lord will take the snakes away,"* rather than that they might be forgiven. God does not bring judgment to His people to be cruel. He brings it so they might learn from it. If God would have complied to the request just to *"take the snakes away,"* it would have defeated the whole purpose of the judgment. So God introduced a piece of art, a sculpture, to teach the Children of Israel a mighty truth of God. The truth of His law and grace, the truth of salvation.

The lesson was taught as follows:

1. If a person is bitten by a snake, he is going to die. The wages of sin is death (Rom. 6:23).

2. They must realize that without help they are going to die — they are in need of salvation.

3. They must seek out the salvation provided, which in their case, is the bronze serpent. The sinner must seek out Jesus.

4. Once they have made the decision of the will, and walk to find the provision of God, they must behold it. It's not good enough just to be in the area of the serpent, they must look upon it. It's not enough for us to be in the church or among Christians. We must know Jesus personally. We must behold His cross.

5. By beholding the serpent they see the judgment of God (the snake), which they must face and thereby face their sin. They must confess their sin even as we do.

6. By beholding the serpent they see the Law of God, but receive the Grace of God and are healed! When we confess and accept the work Jesus did on the cross, we are forgiven and receive the life of His resurrection.

Jesus said of the bronze serpent:

Just as Moses lifted up the snake in the desert, so the Son of Man must be lifted up, that everyone who believes in him may have eternal life (John 3:14-15).

The bronze serpent of the Old Testament was a type of Jesus Christ. A piece of art represented the most important of truths, the salvation of mankind through a restored relationship with God!

THE MISUSE OF THE ARTS

Arts throughout the years have been grossly misused to communicate the negative things of the sinful nature of man and the kingdom of darkness. Many times the arts were glorified and worshiped, and the artists became exulted. To do these things is idolatry worthy of death. Man is to worship God the Creator, and not the created.

They exchanged the truth of God for a lie, and worshiped and served created things rather then the Creator — who is forever praised (Rom. 1:25).

It is sin to worship and adore that which is made. The idolatrous worship of the golden calf (Ex. 32) is an example of such sin (see the chapter on dance for an in-depth study). The result of worshiping art is judgment and death.

The prophets ridiculed those who worship the work of their own hand. Read Isaiah 44:6-23 and Jeremiah 10:11-16. Among other things the following is said:

All who make idols are nothing, and the things they treasure are worthless...craftsmen are nothing but men...(Isa. 44:9,11a).

Both prophets explain the stupidity of worshiping or glorifying the work of a man's hand or an object of his craft. God is the Creator not man. Man just uses the gifts given to him by God. Being talented does not justify pride and elevation. All abilities are given by God. This recognition should make us humble, not arrogant. Art and artists are but an expression of God's creativity through a willing vehicle.

Art, in itself, is neither good nor bad, holy nor unholy. It is the expressed focus of the object of art which determines a godly or ungodly use of an object. A knife can be used for good as well as for evil, to eat with or to kill. The objects of art themselves *"have no breath in them...they are worthless"* (Jer. 10)

I have heard people say that art should be restored, but not the art used today, for it is associated with evil and has its foundation in evil and the world. This is incorrect thinking. All creativity is from God, and creativity is the foundation of any art; for without creativity there is no art. However, the art might be used evilly; in this case it is the use that is wrong, not the misplaced art. When art is used for reasons other than its original purpose, which is to glorify God, we find sin.

The bronze snake of Moses was created to illustrate the law and God's saving grace. It was the tool that was used to bring healing to thousands and became a type of Jesus Christ. As wondrous as this is, the bronze snake is still only a piece of brass.

After Moses used the bronze snake, the Children of Israel kept it among themselves. We don't hear about it again until centuries later, in the reign of King Hezekiah. In the days of Hezekiah, Israel had fallen into idolatry and sin. One of the first things that the King did was to destroy the high places and the objects of idolatrous worship. He then brought back the instruments of David and the true worship of God. Now one would think that the bronze snake might be kept by the Children of Israel as a reminder of their sin and God's salvation from death. One might think that, but it was not the case.

He [King Hezekiah] *removed the high places, smashed the sacred stones and cut down the Asherah poles. He broke into pieces the bronze snake Moses had made, for up to that time the Israelites had been burning incense to it. (It was called Nehushtan* [a piece of brass]) (II Kings 18:4).

The Children of Israel were worshiping the created rather than the Creator. Therefore the bronze snake was completely destroyed. This was the right response to a worthless piece of bronze.

He [Hezekiah] *did what was right in the eyes of the Lord...* (II Kings 18:3).

Here we see that no matter how holy the use of an art has been, being used to glorifying God, the same object can be used to sin against Him. As it has been said: It's not the art, it's how it's used. If an art has fallen into sinful use, the misuse should be dealt with and the sin confronted. However, once you have removed the sin, having dealt with it completely, the art should be restored to its original purpose. We must not allow the misuse of an art to stop us from using art to glorify God, thereby achieving its original purpose (whatever that purpose is). This is clearly seen by the use and misuse of the bronze serpent. Jesus used the bronze snake as an example and type of Himself and of salvation. For this reason the bronze snake was made. Jesus never mentions that the bronze snake had been misused. Why glorify satan's work? Instead He mentions it only as it was intended to be used, as a foreteller of the cross of Jesus Christ and His work of salvation.

Let us likewise, deal with the sin in the arts today; then let us never mention its misuse, restoring it to its original purpose which is to glorify God by showing His beauty, love, grace, judgments and salvation — to bring all people to a greater understanding of God.

THE FINE ARTS

TRUE AND FALSE

1. T F The source of man's creativity is the Spirit of God.

2. T F Scripture supports being excellently skilled and trained in the arts.

3. T F Part of the call of an artist is to train others.

4. T F Art cannot be just beautiful. It must communicate some other scriptural message.

5. T F God used a sculpture to communicate the message of salvation.

6. T F Art, in and of itself, can be classified as holy or unholy.

7. T F The modern arts of today cannot be used to glorify God because they have their roots in sin and are corrupt; they cannot be redeemed.

GROUP DISCUSSION

1. When does an art form cease to glorify God and begin to glorify the flesh or sin? For example, when does the good preacher become an entertainer instead of a teacher, or a musician become a performer instead of a worshiper?

2. How do we view the fine arts? Are they something beyond understanding or an instrument through which God can speak to us? Which should it be? How can we encourage its correct use?

3. How should we encourage the artists of our church and the artistic expression of people in the church, if art is a gift from God and a mighty tool? How have we treated them in the past?

PERSONAL ASSIGNMENT

1. Find someone who you think is talented or artistic and encourage them in the use of their arts for the purposes of God.

2. Write down your gifts and abilities. List how you use them. List how you can better use them and make goals to achieve that end (start by focusing on one gift or talent at a time).

ANSWERS TO THE TRUE AND FALSE

1. T, 2. T, 3. T, 4. F, 5. T, 6. F, 7. F

AFTERWORD

Currently, there is a tremendous worldwide move of the Holy Spirit in Praise and Worship. Christians are experiencing the manifest presence of God in their lives as He dwells in their praise (Psalms 22:3). This rebirth of worship is causing people to be much more expressive in the demonstration of their affection, reverence, and love to the Lord.

For years the church has been silent and still. In 367 A.D., musical instruments and congregational singing were no longer allowed in the church. Only in the last few years have musical instruments been unilaterally accepted by almost every denomination and once again used in the worship experience, all because of a rebirth in the hearts of God's people.

This same renewal in our hearts that has caused the restoration of Biblical praise and worship, has not only caused a rebirth in music, but a rebirth in movement as well. When hearts are changed, new songs come forth; so when that same transformation takes place, one's devotion is often set into motion.

There is much discussion and controversy today over the role of the human body in worship. So there should be. As God reveals new truth, apostolic leaders need to weigh the scriptures and consider what God wants to say to us; then implement it.

Todd Farley, in this book, shared with you the visual side of communication — whether in worship, prayer, prophecy, or teaching. You discovered how God communicated His thoughts through mime, acting, drama, dance and sign, all dramatic expressions of the human body. You saw that Old Testament prophets, like Jeremiah and Ezekiel, often acted out their prophetic burdens. You saw that the worship experience is not only an audible experience but involves the many expressions and postures of the body.

The Bible says that we are to love God, which is the very essence of worship, with all our heart, soul, mind and STRENGTH (Luke 10:27). That involves our bodies. Paul, the Apostle, tells us to "Glorify God in our body" (I Cor. 6:20). Our face, eyes, mouth, hands, arms, and legs all communicate the heart of a worshiper. We are to "show forth the praises of our God" (I Peter 2:9). The posture and actions of our bodies communicate more than our words. That is why God said, "many will see the new song" He put in your mouth, and fear and trust in the Lord (Psalms 40:3).

The visual conveyance is one of the most powerful aspects of communication. It is true "Man looks on the outward appearance" (I Samuel 16:7). That is how God made us. So He also wants us to communicate by our gestures, facial expressions, actions, behavior and body posture.

Having read this book, open your ears to hear what the Lord would speak to you about communication and expression through movement.

LaMar Boschman

For correspondence or booking information write:

MIMEistry International
Todd Farley
9112 Tristan Drive
Garden Grove, CA 92641